Psychology
&Politics

Dr. Rivers.
Dr. William Brown. Dr. Elliot Smith.
Military Hospital, Maghull 1915.

Psychology &Politics

W. H. R. Rivers

With an introduction by Charles S. Myers

 Routledge
Taylor & Francis Group

LONDON AND NEW YORK

First published 2011 by Transaction Publishers

Published 2017 by Routledge
2 Park Square, Milton Park, Abingdon, Oxon OX14 4RN
711 Third Avenue, New York, NY 10017, USA

Routledge is an imprint of the Taylor & Francis Group, an informa business

Library of Congress Catalog Number: 2010038336

Library of Congress Cataloging-in-Publication Data

Rivers, W. H. R. (William Halse Rivers), 1864-1922.
  Psychology and politics / W.H.R. Rivers.
    p. cm.
  Reprint of: Psychology and politics : and other essays / by W. H. R. Rivers, originally published in 1923 by K. Paul, Trench, Trubner & Co., London.
  ISBN 978-1-4128-1819-3 (alk. paper)
    1. Psychology, Applied. 2. Social psychology. 3. Ethnopsychology. I. Title.

BF21.R5 2011
320.01'9-dc22

2010038336

ISBN 13: 978-1-4128-1819-3 (pbk)

PREFATORY NOTE

In January 1922 Dr Rivers was persuaded to accept the invitation to become a candidate for the representation of the University of London in the House of Commons. In his letter of acceptance he wrote : " To one whose life has been passed in scientific research and education the prospect of entering practical politics can be no light matter. But the times are so ominous, the outlook for our own country and the world so black, that if others think I can be of service in political life, I cannot refuse." He at once threw himself with characteristic zeal into the task of expounding his views on politics and of integrating them with his social and psychological convictions, for, he said, " I cannot believe that political problems differ from those of every other aspect of social life in being incapable of solution by scientific methods."

This belief prompted him to deliver the three lectures on psychological theory that are printed in this volume—surely the most remarkable form of appeal to parliamentary electors in the history of politics ! Before his sudden death in June 1922 he had carefully revised the manuscript in a way that indicated his intention to have these lectures published in the form in which they now appear.

Three other addresses are included in this volume, one on Socialism and Human Nature given to the Critical Society less than a fortnight before his death, another on Education and Mental Hygiene, upon the preparation of which he seems to have been engaged at the end, and a lecture on the Aims of Ethnology. During his last three years Dr Rivers delivered this lecture repeatedly in universities and public schools and to a variety of societies of different kinds in Great Britain and America, and refrained from publishing it, because he was able to make use of it whenever he was invited simply to give a lecture at a school, a university, or in fact any kind of gathering of people. Although its connection with politics may not be apparent, it is included in this volume because Dr Rivers approached the problems of politics and education and acquired that wider understanding of the range of psychology and sociology by way of ethnology ; and during the last five years of his life he was constantly pleading for the closer integration of ethnology and psychology. The history of his change of attitude to the problems of ethnology, which he gives in the last chapter of this book, had a direct bearing upon his views on sociology, education and politics. For the clearer vision of the nature of human thought and action and the fuller understanding of the meaning of civilisation that emerged from such studies forcibly impressed upon him the unity of culture and the close interdependence of all mankind, and laid the foundations of his appreciation of what should be the ultimate aim of all government and political action. These addresses are printed without any alterations other than mere typographical corrections.

G. ELLIOT SMITH.

CONTENTS

vii

THE INFLUENCE OF THE LATE W. H. R. RIVERS

By Charles S. Myers, C.B.E., M.D., Sc.D., F.R.S.

THE INFLUENCE OF THE LATE
W. H. R. RIVERS*

WILLIAM HALSE RIVERS RIVERS was born on 12th March 1864, at Luton, near Chatham; the eldest son of the Rev. H. F. Rivers, M.A., formerly of Trinity College, Cambridge, and afterwards vicar of St Faith's, Maidstone, and of Elizabeth, his wife, *née* Hunt. Many of his father's family had been officers in the Navy—a fact responsible, doubtless, for Rivers's love of sea voyages. A relative of his paternal grandfather, Lieut. W. T. Rivers, R.N., was that brave Lieut. William Rivers, R.N., who, as a midshipman in the *Victory* at Trafalgar, was severely wounded in the mouth and had his left leg shot away at the very beginning of the action, in defence of Nelson or in trying to avenge the latter's mortal wound. So at least runs the family tradition ; also according to which Nelson's last words to his surgeon were : " Take care of young Rivers." A maternal uncle of Rivers was Dr James Hunt, who in 1863 founded and was the first President of the Anthropological Society, a precursor of the

* The Presidential Address to the Psychology Section of the British Association, 1922.

xi

Royal Anthropological Institute, and from 1863 to 1866, at the meetings of the British Association, strove to obtain that recognition for anthropology as a distinct Sub-section or Section which was successfully won for Psychology by his nephew, who presided over the Psychological Section of the Association at the Bournemouth meeting in 1919, when the Psychologists were merely a Sub-section of Physiology.

Our " young Rivers " gave his first lecture at the age of twelve, at a debating society of his father's pupils. Its subject was " Monkeys." He was educated first at a preparatory school at Brighton, and from 1877 to 1880 at Tonbridge School. Thence he had hoped to proceed to Cambridge ; but a severe attack of enteric fever compelled him to take a year's rest, and thus prevented him from competing for an entrance scholarship at that University. He matriculated instead in the University of London, and entered St Bartholomew's Hospital in 1882, sharing the intention of one of his father's pupils of becoming an Army doctor. This idea, however, he soon relinquished ; but, like his desire to go to Cambridge, it was to be realised later in life.*

When he took his degree of Bachelor of Medicine in 1886 he was accounted the young-

* For many of the above details of Rivers's early life and antecedents I am indebted to his sister, Miss K. E. Rivers.

est Bachelor ever known at his hospital. Two years later he graduated as Doctor of Medicine, and he spent these two and the two following years in resident appointments at Chichester (1888) and at St Bartholomew's (1889) Hospitals, in a brief period of private medical practice (1890), and in travelling as ship's surgeon to America and Japan (1887), the first of numerous subsequent voyages. In 1891 he became house-physician at the National Hospital, Queen Square, where he first made the acquaintance of Dr Henry Head, whose collaborator he was to be some twenty years later in one of the most striking neurological experiments ever made.

But before he began work at Queen Square, before he assisted Horsley there in his then wonderful operations on the brain, before he met Head fresh from his studies in Germany and enthusiastic over the colour-vision work and novel physiological conceptions of Hering, Rivers had already shown his interest in the study of the mind and the nervous system. Thus, in 1888, when he was twenty-four years of age, we find in the *St Bartholomew's Hospital Reports* (vol. xxiv. pages 249-251) his first published paper on " A Case of Spasm of the Muscles of Neck Causing Protrusion of the Head," and in the following year, in the same *Reports* (vol. xxv. pages 279-280), an abstract of a paper read by him before the Abernethian Society, entitled " Delirium and its Allied Conditions." At this early date he pointed out the analogies between delirium and mania, protested against the use of narcotics in delirium, and condemned the wide separation—too wide even to-day—between diseases of the mind and diseases of the body. In 1891 and in 1893 he read papers to the Abernethian Society, abstracts of which appear in the *St Bartholomew's Hospital Reports* (vol. xxvii. pages 285-286, vol. xxix. page 350), on " Hysteria " and on " Neurasthenia," to which his interests were to return so fruitfully during and after the Great War.

In 1892 he spent the spring and early summer at Jena, attending the lectures of Eucken, Ziehen, Binswanger, and others. In a diary kept by him during this visit to Germany the following sentence occurs : " I have during the last few weeks come to the conclusion that I should go in for insanity when I return to England and work as much as possible at psychology." Accordingly, in the same year he became Clinical Assistant at the Bethlem Royal Hospital, and in 1893 he assisted G. H. Savage in his lectures on mental diseases at Guy's Hospital, laying special stress on their psychological aspect. About the same time, at the request of Professor Sully, he began to lecture on experimental psychology at University College, London.

Meanwhile, at Cambridge, Michael Foster was seeking someone who would give instruction there in the physiology of the sense organs, M'Kendrick having, as Examiner in Physiology, recently complained of the inadequate training of the Cambridge students in this branch of the subject. Foster's choice fell on Rivers, and in 1893 he invited him to the University for this purpose. For a few months Rivers taught simultaneously at Cambridge and at Guy's Hospital and at University College, London. He went to Germany for a short period of study under Professor Kräpelin, then of Heidelberg, whose brilliant analysis of the work curve and careful investigations into the effects of drugs on bodily and mental work had aroused his intense interest. In collaboration with Kräpelin, he carried out a brief investigation into mental fatigue and recovery, published in 1896 (*Journal of Mental Science*, vol. xlii. pages 525-529, and Kräpelin's *Psychologische Arbeiten*, vol. i. pages 627-678), which indicated that even an hour's rest is inadequate to neutralise the fatigue of half an hour's mental work, and paved the way for Rivers's important researches some ten years later upon the effects of drugs on muscular and mental fatigue.

At Cambridge Rivers set himself to plan one of the earliest systematic practical courses in experimental psychology in the world, certainly the first in this country. In 1897 he was officially recognised by the University, being elected to the newly-established Lectureship in Physiological and Experimental Psychology. But the welcome and encouragement he received from cognate branches of study at Cambridge could hardly be called embarrassing. Even to-day practical work is not deemed essential for Cambridge honours candidates in elementary psychology ; psychology is not admitted among the subjects of the Natural Sciences Tripos ; and no provision is made for teaching the subject at Cambridge to medical students. Rivers first turned his attention principally to the study of colour vision and visual space perception. Between 1893 and 1901 he published experimental papers " On Binocular Colour-mixture " (*Proc. Cambs. Philosoph. Soc.*, vol. viii. pages 273-277), on " The Photometry of Coloured Papers " (*Jour. of Physiol.*, vol. xxii. pages 137-145), and " On Erythropsia " (*Trans. Ophthal. Soc., London*, vol. xxi. pages 296-305), and until 1898 he was immersed in the task of mastering the entire literature of past experimental work on vision, the outcome of which was published in 1900 as an article in the second volume of the important *Text-book of Physiology*, edited by Sir Edward Sharpey Schafer.

This exhaustive article of 123 pages on " Vision " by Rivers is still regarded as the most accurate and careful account of the whole subject in the English language. It is of special value, not only as an encyclopædic storehouse of references to the work of previous investigators—although with characteristic modesty Rivers omits to mention himself among them—but also for the unsurpassed critical account of the principal theories of colour vision. In it he displayed the strength and the weakness of Hering's theory and the untenability of Helmholtz's explanations of successive contrast as due to fatigue, and of simultaneous contrast as due to psychological factors. Rivers clearly showed that the effect of psychological factors is not to create but to mask the phenomena of simultaneous contrast, which are really dependent on what he terms " the physiological reciprocity of adjoining retinal areas." His enthusiasm for Hering's theories led him to give by far the most detailed presentation of them that had then or has since appeared in our language. In classifying the phenomena of red-green colour-blindness, on which Helmholtz largely based his trichromic theory, Rivers proposed the useful terms " scoterythrous " and " photerythrous " in place of the terms " protanopic " and " deuteranopic," so as to avoid, in describing these phenomena, the use of names which implied the acceptance of a particular theory of colour vision. These terms have failed, however, to obtain general adoption.

In 1896 Rivers published an important paper " On the Apparent Size of Objects " (*Mind*, N.S., vol. v. pages 71-80), in which he described his investigations into the effects of atropin and eserin on the size of seen objects. He distinguished two kinds of micropsia which had hitherto been confused— micropsia at the fixation-point due to irradiation, and micropsia beyond the fixation-point, which is of special psychological importance. Rivers came to the interesting conclusion that the mere effort to carry out a movement of accommodation may produce the same micropsia as when that effort is actually followed by movement. In other words, an illusion of size may be dependent solely on central factors. His later work, in conjunction with Professor Dawes Hicks, on " The Illusion of Compared Horizontal and Vertical Lines," which was published in 1908 (*Brit. Jour. of Psychol.*, vol. ii. pages 241-260), led him to trace this illusion to origins still less motor in nature. Here horizontal and vertical lines were compared under tachistoscopic and under prolonged exposure. The momentary view of the lines in the tachistoscope precluded any movement or effort of movement of the eyes, which had been supposed by many to be responsible for the over-estimation of vertical lines owing to the greater difficulty of eye movement in the vertical as compared with the horizontal direction. The amount of the illusion was found to be approximately the same for tachistoscopic as for prolonged exposure of the lines, but in the tachistoscopic exposure the judgment was more definite and less hesitating—in other words, more naïve, more purely sensory, more " physiological "—than in prolonged exposure. This result, which led to further work by Dr E. O. Lewis at Cambridge under Rivers upon the Müller-Lyer illusion and upon the comparison of " filled " and " empty " space, is of fundamental physiological importance. Although it is not inconsistent with the view that visual space perception depends *for its genesis* on eye movement, it compels us to admit that visual space perception, *once acquired*, can occur in the absence of eye movement ; or, in more general language, that changes in consciousness, originally arising in connection with muscular activity, may later occur in the absence of that activity. The provision of experimental evidence in favour of so fundamental and wide-reaching a view is obviously of the greatest importance.

In 1898, in which year he was given the degree of Hon. M.A. at Cambridge, Rivers took a fresh path in his varied career by accepting Dr A. C. Haddon's invitation to join the Cambridge Anthropological Expedition to the Torres Straits. This was the first expedition in which systematic work was carried out in the ethnological application of the methods and apparatus of experimental psychology. His former pupils, Prof. W. M'Dougall and I, assisted Rivers in this new field. Rivers interested himself especially in investigating the vision of the natives—their visual acuity, their colour vision, their colour nomenclature, and their susceptibility to certain visual geometric illusions. He continued to carry out psychological work of the same comparative ethnological character after his return from the Torres Straits in Scotland (where he and I sought comparative data), during a visit to Egypt in the winter of 1900, and from 1901-2 in his expedition to the Todas of Southern India.

The Torres Straits expedition marked a turning-point in Rivers's life interests, as they were for the first time directed towards ethnological studies, to which he became ardently devoted ever after, until his death removed one who at the time was President of the Royal Anthropological Institute, had in 1920-1 been President of the Folk Lore Society, and had in 1911 been President of the Section of Anthropology of the British Association. His ethnological and sociological work during his expedition to the Todas and during his two subsequent expeditions to Melanesia is too well known to need mention here. It was Rivers's own view that his most important contributions to science are to be found in the two volumes of his *History of Melanesian Society*, published in 1914.

His psychological investigations among the Torres Straits islanders, Egyptians, and Todas (*Reports of the Cambridge Anthrop. Exped. to Torres Straits*, vol. ii. Pt. I. pages 1-132 ; *Jour. of Anthrop. Inst.*, vol. xxxi. pages 229-247 ; *Brit. Jour. of Psychol.*, vol. i. pages 321-396) will ever stand as models of precise, methodical observations in the field of ethnological psychology. Nowhere does he disclose more clearly the admirably scientific bent of his mind—his insistence of scientific procedure, his delight in scientific analysis, and his facility in adapting scientific methods to novel experimental conditions. He reached the conclusion that no substantial difference exists between the visual acuity of civilised and uncivilised peoples, and that the latter show a very definite diminution in sensibility to blue, which, as he suggested, is perhaps attributable to the higher macular pigmentation among coloured peoples. He observed a generally defective nomenclature for blue, green, and brown among primitive peoples, both white and coloured, and large differences in the frequency of colour-blindness among the different uncivilised peoples whom he examined. In his work on visual illusions he found that the vertical-horizontal-line illusion was more marked, while the Müller-Lyer illusion was less marked, among un-

civilised than among civilised communities;
and he concluded that the former illusion
was therefore dependent rather on physiological, the latter rather on psychological
factors, the former being counteracted, the
latter being favoured, by previous experience
—*e.g.* of drawing lines or of apprehending
complex figures as wholes.

In 1903, the year after his return from
India, and the year of his election to a Fellow-
ship at St John's College, Rivers began an
investigation, continued for five years, with
Dr Henry Head, in which the latter, certain
sensory nerves of whose arm had been experi-
mentally divided, acted as subject, and Rivers
acted as experimenter, applying various
stimuli to the arm and recording the phenomena of returning cutaneous sensibility. The
results of this heroic and lengthy investigation are well known. The discovery of a
crude punctate protopathic sensibility, distinct from a more refined epicritic sensibility,
so deeply impressed Rivers that a decade
later his psychological views may be said to
have been centred round this distinction
between the ungraded, " all-or-nothing," dif-
fusely localising functions of the protopathic
system, and the delicately graded, discriminative, accurately localising functions of the
epicritic system. The exact interpretation
of this " Human Experiment in Nerve
Division," published at length in 1908 (*Brain*,

vol. xxxi. pages 323-450), has been disputed by subsequent workers, whose divergent results, however, are at least partly due to their employment of different methods of procedure. Head's experiment has never been identically repeated, and until this has been done we are probably safe in trusting to the results reached by the imaginative genius and the cautious critical insight of this rare combination of investigators. At a far higher nervous level broad analogies to this peripheral analysis of cutaneous sensibility were later found by Head when thalamic came to be compared with cortical activity and sensibility.

While working with Head upon his arm, Rivers's indomitable activity led him to simultaneous occupation in other fields. In 1904 he assisted Professor James Ward to found and to edit the *British Journal of Psychology*, and in that year he also received an invitation to deliver the Croonian Lectures in 1906 at the Royal College of Physicians, of which in 1899 he had been elected a Fellow. The study of drug effects had long interested him. In a paper on " Experimental Psychology in Relation to Insanity," read before the Medico-Psychological Society in 1895 (*Lancet*, vol. lxxiii. page 867), he had drawn the attention of psychiatrists to the comparability of drug effects with the early stages of mental disorders before they were seen by the physician. And so, reverting to the work he had done under Kräpelin many years previously, he chose as his subject for the Croonian Lectures " The Influence of Alcohol and other Drugs on Fatigue " (Arnold, 1908). But although he utilised Kräpelin's ergograph and many of Kräpelin's methods, Rivers's *flair* for discovering previous " faulty methods of investigation " and his devotion to scientific methods and accuracy could not fail to advance the subject. Of no one may it be more truly said than of him—*nihil tetigit quod non ornavit*. He felt instinctively that many of the supposed effects of alcohol were really due to the suggestion, interest, excitement, or sensory stimulation accompanying the taking of the drug. Accordingly he disguised the drug, and prepared a control mixture which was indistinguishable from it. On certain days the drug mixture was taken, on other days the control mixture was taken, the subject never knowing which he was drinking. Rivers engaged Mr H. N. Webber as a subject who could devote himself to the investigation so completely as to lead the necessarily uniform life while it was being carried out. He found that the sudden cessation of all tea and coffee necessary for the study of the effects of caffeine induced a loss of energy, and that other mental disturbance might occur through giving up all forms of alcoholic drink. Therefore most of his experiments were carried out more than twelve months after the taking of these drinks had been discontinued. Instead of recording a single ergogram, Rivers took several sets of ergograms each day, each set consisting usually of six ergograms taken at intervals of two minutes, and separated from the next set by an interval of thirty or sixty minutes. He arranged that the drug mixture or the control mixture should be taken after obtaining the first set of ergograms, which served as a standard wherewith subsequent sets on the same day might be compared. He worked with Mr Webber on alcohol and caffeine, and his research was followed by the similar work of Dr P. C. V. Jones in 1908 on strychnine, and of Dr J. G. Slade in 1909 on Liebig extract.

With these vast improvements in method, Rivers failed to confirm the conclusions of nearly all earlier investigators on the effects of from 5 to 20 c.c. of absolute alcohol on muscular work. His results with these doses, alike for muscular and mental work, were mainly negative, and indeed with larger doses (40 c.c.) were variable and inconclusive ; although an equivalent quantity of whisky gave an immediate increase of muscular work—a result which strongly suggests the influence of sensory stimulation rather than the direct effect of the drug on the central nervous system or on the muscular tissues.

Rivers concluded that alcohol may in some conditions favourably act on muscular work by increasing pleasurable emotion and by dulling sensations of fatigue, but that probably its most important effect is to depress higher control, thus tending to increase muscular and to diminish mental efficiency. Working with caffeine, Rivers also obtained effects much less pronounced than those recorded by several earlier observers. He adduced evidence to indicate that (like alcohol) caffeine has a double action on muscular activity, the one immediately increasing the *height* of the contractions obtained and persisting, the other producing an initial slow, transitory increase in the *number* of the contractions, and then a fall. Following Kräpelin, he suggested that the former action represents a peripheral, the latter a central effect.

He also put forward novel suggestions as to the true course of the fatigue curve, and laid stress on the importance of carrying out ergographic work by peripheral electrical stimulation. These views are certain to bear fruit in the future. Indeed, it may be safely said that no one can henceforth afford to investigate the effect of drugs on the intact organism without first mastering Rivers's work on the subject.

From the concluding passages of these Croonian Lectures the following sentences may be aptly cited : " The branch of psychology in which I am chiefly interested is that to which the name of individual psychology is usually given. It is that branch of psychology which deals with the differences in the mental constitutions of different peoples, and by an extension of the term to the differences which characterise the members of different races. . . . These experiments leave little doubt that variations in the actions of drugs on different persons may have their basis in deep-seated physiological variations, and I believe that the study of these variations of susceptibility may do more than perhaps any other line of work to enable us to understand the nature of temperament and the relation between the mental and physical characters which form its two aspects."

Rivers's interests did not lie in the collection of masses of heterogeneous data, in obtaining blurred averages from vast numbers of individuals, in concocting mathematical devices, or in applying mathematical formulæ to the numerical data thus accumulated ; they lay throughout his varied career in studying and analysing individual mental differences, in getting to know the individual in his relation to his environment. In ordinary circumstances, as he later said, " There is too little scope for the variations of conditions which is the essence of experiment. . . . While the experimental method as applied to the normal adult has borne little fruit, it would be difficult to rate too highly the importance of experiment in discovering and testing methods to be used in other lines of psychological inquiry where a wider variation of conditions is present " (*Brit. Jour. of Psychol.*, vol. x. page 185).

It was the importance of studying the play of the most variable conditions that led Rivers to investigate, as we have seen, first racial mental differences, then the differences produced in a given individual by nerve section, and finally those produced in different individuals by different drugs. Throughout his life he was steadfast to the biological standpoint, correlating the psychological with the physiological, and hoping to discover different mental levels corresponding to different neural levels.

And so we approach the last phase of Rivers's psychological work, the outcome of his war experiences. In 1907 he had given up his University teaching in experimental psychology ; for six years before the war he had published nothing of psychological or physiological interest. This was a period in which Rivers devoted himself wholly to the ethnology and sociology of primitive peoples. The outbreak of war found him for the second time visiting Melanesia for ethnological field work. Failing at first to get war work on his return to England,

Rivers set himself to prepare the Fitzpatrick Lectures on " Medicine, Magic, and Religion," which he had been invited to deliver to the Royal College of Physicians of London in 1915 and 1916. In 1915 his psychological and ethnological researches were recognised by the award to him of a Royal Medal by the Royal Society, of which he had been elected a Fellow in 1908. In July 1915 he went as medical officer to the Maghull War Hospital, near Liverpool, and in 1916 to the Craiglockhart War Hospital, Edinburgh, receiving a commission in the R.A.M.C. In these hospitals he began the work on the psychoneuroses that led him to his studies of the unconscious and of dreams, which resulted in his well-known book, *Instinct and the Unconscious*, published first in 1920 (already in a second edition), and in a practically completed volume on *Conflict and Dream*, which is to be published posthumously. From 1917 he acted as consulting psychologist to the Royal Air Force, being attached to the Central Hospital at Hampstead.

This period not merely marks a new phase in Rivers's work, but is also characterised by a distinct change in his personality and writings. In entering the Army and in investigating the psychoneuroses he was fulfilling the desires of his youth. Whether through the realisation of such long-discarded or suppressed wishes, or through other causes

—*e.g.* the gratified desire of an opportunity for more sympathetic insight into the mental life of his fellows—he became another and a far happier man. Diffidence gave place to confidence, hesitation to certainty, reticence to outspokenness, a somewhat laboured literary style to one remarkable for its ease and charm. Over forty publications can be traced to these years, between 1916 and the date of his death. It was a period in which his genius was released from its former shackles, in which intuition was less controlled by intellectual doubt, in which inspiration brought with it the usual accompaniment of emotional conviction—even an occasional impatience with those who failed to accept his point of view. But his honest, generous character remained unchanged to the last. Ever willing to devote himself unsparingly to a cause he believed right, or to give of his best to help a fellow-being in mental distress, he worked with an indomitable self-denying energy, won the gratitude and affection of numberless nerve-shattered soldier-patients, whom he treated with unsurpassed judgment and success, and attracted all kinds of people to this new aspect of psychology. Painters, poets, authors, artisans, all came to recognise the value of his work, to seek, to win, and to appreciate his sympathy and his friendship. It was characteristic of his thoroughness that while attached to the Royal

Air Force he took numerous flights, " looping the loop " and performing other trying evolutions in the air, so that he might gain adequate experience of flying and be able to treat his patients and to test candidates satisfactorily. He had the courage to defend much of Freud's new teaching at a time when it was carelessly condemned *in toto* by those in authority, who were too ignorant or too incompetent to form any just opinion of its undoubted merits and undoubted defects. He was prepared to admit the importance of the conflict of social factors with the sexual instincts in certain psychoneuroses of civil life, but in the psychoneuroses of warfare and of occupations like mining he believed that the conflicting instincts were not sexual, but were the danger instincts, related to the instinct of self-preservation.

Thus in the best sense of the term Rivers became a man of the world, and no longer a man of the laboratory and of the study. He found time to serve on the Medical Research Council's Air Medical Investigation Committee, on its Mental Disorders Committee, on its Miners' Nystagmus Committee, and on the Psychological Committee of its Industrial Fatigue Research Board. He served on a committee, of ecclesiastical complexion, appointed to inquire into the new psychotherapy, and he had many close friends among the missionaries, to whom he gave and from whom he received assistance in the social and ethnological side of their work.

In 1919, in which year he received honorary degrees from the Universities of St Andrews and Manchester, he returned to Cambridge as Prælector in Natural Sciences at St John's College, and began immediately to exercise a wonderful influence over the younger members of the University by his fascinating lectures, his " Sunday evenings," and, above all, by his ever-ready interest and sympathy. As he himself wrote, after the war work, " which brought me into contact with the real problems of life . . . I felt that it was impossible for me to return to my life of detachment." And when a few months before his death he was invited by the Labour Party to a still more public sphere of work, viz. to become a Parliamentary candidate representing the University of London, once again he gave himself unsparingly. He wrote at the time : " To one whose life has been passed in scientific research and education the prospect of entering practical politics can be no light matter. But the times are so ominous, the outlook both for our own country and the world so black, that if others think I can be of service in political life I cannot refuse." On several occasions subsequently he addressed interested London audiences, consisting largely of his supporters,

INFLUENCE OF W. H. R. RIVERS

on the relations between Psychology and Politics.

Rivers's views on the so-called herd-instinct were the natural outcome of those which he had put forward during the preceding five years and collected together in his *Instinct and the Unconscious*. His aim in writing this book was, as he says, "to provide a biological theory for the psychoneuroses," to view the psychological from the physiological standpoint. He maintained that an exact correspondence holds between the inhibition of the physiologist and the repression of the psychologist. He regarded mental disorders as mainly dependent on the coming to the surface of older activities which had been previously controlled or suppressed by the later products of evolution. Here Rivers went beyond adopting Hughlings Jackson's celebrated explanation of the phenomena of nervous diseases as arising largely from the release of lower-level activities from higher-level controls. He further supposed that these lower-level activities represent earlier racial activities held more or less in abeyance by activities later acquired. This conception he derived from his work with Henry Head on cutaneous sensibility. Rivers could see but "two chief possibilities" of interpreting the phenomena disclosed in the study of Head's arm. Either epicritic sensibility is protopathic sensibility in greater perfection, or else protopathic sensibility and epicritic sensibility represent two distinct stages in the development of the nervous system. Failing to see any other explanation, he adopted the second of these alternatives. He supposed that at some period of evolution, when epicritic sensibility, with its generally surface distribution, its high degree of discrimination, and its power of accurate localisation, made its appearance, the previously existing protopathic sensibility, with its punctate distribution, its " all-or-nothing " character, and its broad radiating localisation, became in part inhibited or " suppressed," in part blended or " fused " with the newly-acquired sensibility so as to form a useful product. He supposed that the suppressed portion persisted in a condition of unconscious existence, and he emphasised the biological importance of suppression. He considered at first that the protopathic sensibility " has all the characters we associate with instinct," whereas the later epicritic sensibility has the characters of intelligence or reason. So he came to hold that instinct " led the animal kingdom a certain distance in the line of progress," whereupon " a new development began on different lines," " starting a new path, developing a new mechanism which utilised such portions of the old as suited its purpose."

Evolutio per saltus was thus the keynote of Rivers's views on mental development. Just as the experience of the caterpillar or tadpole is for the most part suppressed in the experience of the butterfly or frog, so instinctive reactions tend to be suppressed in intelligent experience whenever the immediate and unmodifiable nature of the one becomes incompatible with the diametrically opposite characters of the other. Just as parts of the protopathic fuse with the later acquired epicritic sensibility, so parts of our early experience, of which other parts are suppressed, fuse with later experience in affecting adult character. " Experience," he explained, " becomes unconscious because instinct and intelligence run on different lines, and are in many respects incompatible with one another."

Rivers was compelled later to recognise " epicritic " characters in certain instincts. He came to suppose that " the instincts connected with the needs of the individual " and with the early preservation of the race are mainly " of the protopathic kind," whereas the epicritic group of instincts first appeared with the development of gregarious life. He recognised the epicritic form of mental activity in the instincts connected with the social life, especially of insects, and also in the states of hypnosis and sleep. Finally, he doubted the validity of the usual distinctions between instinct and intelligence.

Throughout his work on this wide subject Rivers endeavoured to give a strict definition to words which had hitherto been ambiguously or loosely used. He defined *unconscious experience* as that which is incapable of being brought into the field of consciousness save under such special conditions as "sleep, hypnosis, the method of free association, and certain pathological states." He defined *repression* as the self-active, "witting" expulsion of experience from consciousness, and *suppression* as the "unwitting" process by which experience becomes unconscious. Thus suppression may occur without repression. When one refuses to consider an alternative path of action, one represses it; when a memory becomes "of itself" inaccessible to recall, it is suppressed. When such a suppressed experience acquires an independent activity which carries with it an independent consciousness, it undergoes, according to Rivers's usage of the term, *dissociation*. Thus suppression may occur without dissociation. In its most perfect form, according to Rivers, suppression is illustrated by the instinct of immobility which forms one of the reactions to danger; the fugue (as also somnambulism) is "a typical and characteristic instance of dissociation."

From his point of view Rivers was naturally led, wherever possible, to interpret abnormal mental conditions in terms of regression to more primitive, hitherto suppressed activities. He held that the hysterias are essentially

" substitution neuroses," connected with and modified by the gregarious instincts, and are primarily due to a regression to the primitive instinctive danger reaction of immobility, greatly modified by suggestion. So, too, he held that the anxiety neuroses, which are for him essentially " repression neuroses," also show regression, though less complete, in the strength and frequency of emotional reaction, in the failure during states of phantasy to appreciate reality, in the reversion to the nightmares, and especially the terrifying animal dreams, characteristic of childhood, in the occurrence of compulsory acts, in the desire for solitude, etc. Indeed, because he believed that suppression is especially apt to occur, and to be relatively or absolutely perfect, in infancy, Rivers suggested that the independent activity of suppressed experience and the process of dissociation, as exemplified in fugues, complexes, etc., are themselves examples of regression.

He criticised Freud's conception of the censorship, substituting in place of that anthropomorphically - coloured sociological parallel the physiological and non-teleological conception of regression. He supposed the mimetic, fantastic and symbolic forms in which hysterias and dreams manifest themselves to be natural to the infantile stages of human development, individual or collective. For him they were examples of regression to low-level characters, and not, as Freud supposes, ascribable to compromise formations to elude the vigilance of an all-protective censor. He regarded nightmares and war-dreams as examples of infantile states. He believed the absence of effect in many normal dreams to be natural to the infantile attitude, which would treat the situation in question with indifference. That absence of effect also arises from the harmless symbolic solution of the conflict. The affect of dreams is only painful, Rivers supposed, when they fail to provide a solution of the conflict, and is not due, as Freud holds, to the activity of the censor. In the social behaviour of primitive communities Rivers was able to find striking analogies to the characteristics of dreams, as described by Freud.

On the protopathic side he ranged the primitive instincts and emotions, and the complexes, together with the activities of the optic thalamus, and on the epicritic side intelligence and the sentiments, together with the activities of the cerebral cortex. We are now in a position to examine Rivers's treatment of the gregarious behaviour of animal and human life, on which he was still engaged at the time of his death. In the gregarious instinct he recognised a cognitive aspect which he termed " intuition," an affective aspect which he termed " sympathy," and a motor aspect which he termed "mimesis." He used "mimesis" for the process of imitation so far as it was unwitting. "Sympathy" he regarded as always unwitting. "Intuition" he defined as the process whereby one person is unwittingly influenced by another's cognitive activity. But I feel sure that the term "unwittingly" is not to be considered here as equivalent to "telepathically." All that Rivers meant was that the person is influenced by certain stimuli without appreciating their nature and meaning. He preferred to employ the term "suggestion" as covering all the processes by which one mind acts on or is acted on by another unwittingly. He supposed that in the course of mental evolution epicritic characters displaced the early protopathic characters of instinctive behaviour owing to the incidence of gregarious life, especially among insects, and owing to the appearance and development of intelligence, especially in man. The suggestion inherent in gregarious behaviour implies some graduation of mental and bodily activity—an instinctive and unwitting discrimination distinct from the witting discrimination of intelligence. Suggestion, in primitive gregarious behaviour, as also in the dissociated state of hypnosis, and in its allied form, ordinary sleep, is prevented if witting processes be active ; it " is a process of the unconscious," said Rivers. Both within the herd and during hypnosis, which he believed to be fundamentally of a collective nature, sensibility is heightened, so that the organism may be able to react to minute and almost imperceptible stimuli. Had he lived, Rivers would have carried this conception of the evolution of gregarious life still further by distinguishing between the more lowly leaderless herd and the herd which has acquired a definite leader. He would have traced the development of the new affect of submission and of the new behaviour of obedience to the leader, and he would doubtless have accredited the leader with the higher affects of superiority and felt prestige, with the higher cognition that comes of intuitive foresight, and with the higher behaviour of intuitive adaptation, initiative and command. I expect, too, that he would have sketched the development of still later forms of social activity, complicated by the interaction and combination of intellectual and instinctive processes—the witting deliberations and decisions on the part of the leader, and the intellectual understanding of the reasons for their confidence in him and for their appropriate behaviour on the part of those who are led.

But it would be idle further to speculate on the ideas of which we have been robbed by Rivers's untimely death. Let us rather console ourselves with the vast amount of valuable and suggestive material which he has left behind and with the stimulating memories of one who, despite the fact that his health was never robust, devoted himself unsparingly to scientific work and to the claims of any deserving human beings or of any deserving humane cause that were made upon him. There are, no doubt, some who believe that Rivers's earlier experimental psychological work—on vision, on the effects of drugs, and on cutaneous sensibility—is likely to be more lasting than his later speculations on the nature of instinct, the unconscious, dreams, and the psychoneuroses. No one can doubt the scientific permanence of his investigations in the laboratory or in the field ; they are a standing monument to us of thoroughness and accuracy combined with criticism and genius. But even those who hesitate to suppose that at some definite period in mental evolution intelligence suddenly made its appearance and was grafted on to instinct, or that epicritic sensibility was suddenly added to a mental life which had before enjoyed only protopathic sensibility—even those who may not see eye to eye with Rivers on these and other fundamental views on which much of his later work rested will be foremost in recognising the extraordinarily stimulating, suggestive, and fruitful character of all that he poured forth with such astounding speed and profusion during the closing years of his life.

And, above all, we mourn a teacher who was not merely a man of science devoted to abstract problems, but who realised the value of and took a keen delight in applying the knowledge gained in his special subject to more real and living problems of a more concrete, practical, everyday character. Rivers's careful methods of investigating cutaneous sensibility and the *rationale* of his successful treatment of the psychoneuroses were directly due to his psychological training. So, too, his epoch-making discoveries and his views in the field of anthropology on the spread and conflict of cultures were largely due to the application of that training. Shortly before his death he was developing, as a committee member of the Industrial Fatigue Research Board, an intense interest in that youngest application of psychology, viz. to the improvement of human conditions in industrial and commercial work by the methods of experimental psychology applied to fatigue study, motion study, and vocational selection.

Unhappily, men of such wide sympathies and understanding as Rivers, combined with a devotion to scientific work, are rare. He himself recognised that " specialisation has . . . in recent years reached such a pitch that it has become a serious evil. There is even a tendency," he rightly said, " to regard with suspicion one who betrays the possession of knowledge or attainments outside a narrow circle of interests " (*Brit. Jour. of Psychol.*, vol. x. page 184). Let his life, his wisdom, his wide interests, sympathies and attainments, and the generosity and honesty of his character, be an example to us in our common object—the Advancement of Science.

PSYCHOLOGY AND POLITICS

I

PSYCHOLOGY AND POLITICS

I AM afraid that I have been unduly bold in undertaking the task of speaking about the relation between psychology and politics. Probably most of you are hoping that I may be able to utilise such psychological knowledge as we possess to point the way towards a solution of some of the many thorny political problems with which we are now confronted. Though it is possible that I may be able to go some little way in this direction, I wish to begin this course of lectures by asking you not to expect too much, and by pointing out some of the obstacles in the way of fulfilling the purpose at which we should all wish to aim.

The first point on which to insist is that the science of psychology is still very young ; in so far as concerns the kind of problem with which we are now concerned, it can hardly be said to be yet in its teens. We all recognise now that the art of government is far more than a matter ruled by intellect, and yet until quite recently the psychologist was interested in little else. Until recently he paid but scant attention to the affective aspect of mental life, to the instincts with which this aspect is so closely linked, and to the vast store of experience which is capable of influencing our thoughts and actions, though it is not readily, or may be even only with the greatest difficulty accessible, to consciousness. These realms of mental experience and activity are of so vague and indefinite a kind as compared with intellectual processes that their study did not appeal to men who had been trained, as nearly all psychologists then were, in the intellectual exercises of logic or the subtle distinctions and verbal refinements of metaphysics. As a shocking example of the neglect of the less intellectual aspects of psychology I am able to quote myself. So recently as just before the war, less than ten years ago, I was one of those concerned in drawing up a syllabus for an examination in psychology, and what makes the matter worse, for an examination intended for those who wished to specialise in psychological medicine. When, after the war, we had to undertake a revision of this syllabus, I discovered to my horror that the heading of instinct had not been included. So little did instinct occupy our thoughts in those days that we had neglected the subject even when prescribing a course of psychological study in a case where its importance is now so obvious that it seems incredible it could be omitted. And now we all recognise that in many other departments of mental activity the instincts, the affective states associated with them, and the sentiments of which they form the basis, are all factors of the greatest importance in the determination of human behaviour, and especially behaviour of that social kind of which political behaviour is only a special branch. At the present moment, as seems always to happen when experience leads people to correct a fault, the pendulum has swung, or is swinging, too far in the opposite direction, so that there is now a tendency to underestimate the importance of the intellectual factors in the determination of human conduct. It is only gradually that we shall come to see just how intelligence and the intellectual factor take their part in controlling and directing the more affective elements, and how the ultimate factors upon which sane conduct, whether of individual or group, depends are those in which the basic instinctive elements have been modified by reason.

In this state of uncertainty in which a young, almost indeed an embryo, science finds itself, one should be chary of attempting to apply its findings practically. There is now a serious danger that psychology will fall into discredit, partly owing to the zeal of its votaries for the unconscious and infantile aspects of the mind, but still more owing to premature attempts to utilise its supposed discoveries practically while the basis upon which they rest is uncertain and insecure. It seems to me almost certain that there will be a reaction against the almost universal interest which the study of psychology excites to-day, and that we are approaching a period when it may even become a matter of ridicule to make those references to psychological explanation and interpretation which now arouse such hopes and interest.

Animated as I am by these apprehensions concerning the immediate value—I have no doubts whatever concerning the ultimate value —of psychology in politics, I have no intention of adding to the gravity of the approaching reaction by too ambitious attempts to show how psychological doctrines can be immediately applied to the solution of political problems.

In these lectures I shall deal in the main with certain general principles and shall state problems rather than attempt their solution. Though at the same time I confess to the belief that if it is possible to state a problem clearly and unequivocally, one has already gone a long way towards its solution.

In beginning the consideration of my subject after this preliminary warning, I must first stress the fact that in applying psychology to the field of politics, we shall be dealing with social or collective psychology rather than with the psychology of the individual. This at once raises a whole group of problems, some of a most difficult kind, concerning the relation between individual and collective psychology, such problems as the concept of a collective or group mind, together with the question how far society can be regarded as an organism, and the explanation of the fact that when a number of individuals act together, the product of their combined activity is not the same as that which would have emerged from the separate activity of the individuals, even if the products of their individual activity were synthesised by some external agent. With some of these matters I shall attempt to deal in the course of these lectures, and I now propose to proceed to a problem of a fundamental kind which confronts the psychologist who turns from the study of the individual to that of the group.

In a paper written in 1914, but owing to the occurrence of the war not published until two years later,* I have considered the relation between psychology and sociology, putting forward the position that our chief avenue to the formulation of an adequate science of social psychology lies in the observation of social conduct, including under this heading not merely the social conduct of

* "Sociology and Psychology," *Sociological Review*, 1916, vol. ix. page 1.

everyday life, but still more those forms of it which are subsumed under the headings of religion, economics and politics, as well as the social institution of language. Though I did not use the term "behaviourism," the point of view put forward in that paper was that in order to understand the real springs of social conduct we have to adopt the attitude of the behaviourist. I put forward the view that the social behaviour of mankind is capable of being studied as a methodological principle, independently of the psychological basis of that behaviour, forming a discipline which might be called "pure sociology," and that such a discipline would give us a firm basis for the study of social psychology. In illustration of my point I took the relation between the social institution of war as studied comparatively and the emotion of revenge which had been especially emphasised by Professor Westermarck. In his book on *The Origin and Development of the Moral Ideas* * this writer had assumed at the outset that especially that form of warfare known as the blood-feud was the result of the activity of the emotion of revenge, and had then proceeded to cite in favour of this position a number of examples of warfare from various parts of the world, apparently believing them to support his position when, as a matter of fact, a number of them directly

* London, 1906, vol. i. page 477.

contradicted it. Thus, to take only one example, Professor Westermarck cites in favour of his thesis that the blood-feud is determined by revenge cases in which the "revenge" takes the form of adopting the murderer into the family and treating him as one of its members. Judging from his most recent work * Professor Westermarck seems to be unable to see that such social behaviour does not readily fit in with the dependence of the blood-feud on revenge. If we start from behaviour of this kind we shall be driven to formulate motives more complicated than the simple emotion of revenge put forward by Professor Westermarck. Even if revenge remains of our chief interest, we need some different mode of treatment if we are to discover how far revenge is a universal character of the human mind; how far, if universal, it has developed, atrophied and been modified in the course of human history; and whether, if universal, it is an emotion which has the same content and character among different peoples or varies with the physical and social environment. These questions do not involve idle academical distinctions, but are of the greatest possible importance. Thus, if it could be shown that revenge is not a universal human character, it would follow that it is not in-

* *The History of Human Marriage*, 5th edition, 1921, vol. i. page 9.

stinctive, or if instinctive, that it is either the expression of an instinct only recently acquired or, if deeply seated, that it is capable of being successfully suppressed. In either case we should be in a far more hopeful position so far as the eradication of war is concerned than if revenge is the primary, deeply seated, universal instinct which it is assumed to be by Professor Westermarck.

In the further course of the paper I am considering, I showed that though it was theoretically possible to have a science of pure, or as it might be more suitably termed inductive, sociology, this was not possible so long as this science takes its terminology from the language of everyday life with its inevitable psychological implications, and that the two lines of study of pure sociology and social psychology, or of inductive and deductive sociology, should go on side by side, and that the student should recognise clearly which of the two methods he is following.

The general conclusion to which I was led is that at the present stage of our inquiry, and probably for a long time to come, the student of pure or inductive sociology is, and will be, able to do far more for a science of social psychology, than at present, or for some time, the psychologist can do for a science of sociology. The observation of social behaviour must for long be our chief instrument towards the formulation of a science of collective psychology.

I am afraid that it may seem a somewhat depressing introduction to a course of lectures on psychology and politics to begin with such a statement concerning the science of sociology which includes politics in its scope. The paper to which I have referred was written eight years ago, and though as a statement of method I believe that it still holds good, the science of psychology has advanced greatly in the interval, or perhaps more correctly, certain psychological doctrines which were then little known have now become the subject of almost universal interest, though not, I am afraid, of universal understanding. I propose in this course to consider whether these advances in knowledge have made it more possible now than eight years ago to apply psychological doctrines directly to the solution of any of the practical problems of politics.

In considering the relation between psychology and the comprehensive science of sociology of which the study of politics forms part, I have taken as an example the relation between the social institution of warfare and the emotion of revenge. I propose now to give some examples of the same kind of principle which come more definitely into the realm of political science. Before doing so, however, I may refer to a problem of fundamental importance which has a definite bearing on our subject. Our existing psychological knowledge is derived from the study of the individual; from the observation or introspection of the mental processes of the more or less normal individual in the first place, and in the second place by the observation from without, combined in favourable cases with conclusions gained from introspection, of the individual under abnormal conditions, and especially when afflicted by disease, and during the development of childhood. A great deal of so-called " social psychology " consists in the direct application of the conclusions of this psychology of the individual to collective behaviour on the assumption, tacit or avowed, that since society consists of individuals, what is true of the individual must necessarily be true of the group of individuals. I propose to consider this problem at a later stage and only mention it now as another reason why it is necessary to study social behaviour as an independent discipline, for I believe that such a question as that I have just put is not going to be answered on *a priori* grounds, but that a satisfactory answer will only be reached by the study of evidence in which the behaviour of the individual is compared with the behaviour of the group. For the moment I must be content to mention this problem and ask you to bear it in mind while you follow me in a brief inquiry into the relation between motive and behaviour in certain departments of politics.

I will take as my first example the institution of female suffrage. Among the mass of conflicting motives which prompted the long struggle concerning this political institution in our own and other countries, one which was absent was any definite body of knowledge worthy of being called scientific, concerning the existence of psychological differences between men and women in respect of the capacity to govern. Works in which the psychological character of the two sexes were compared dealt largely with observations on such subjects as sense-acuity and speed of reaction, which have no obvious connection, probably none at all, with the far more subtle factors which come into play in the exercise of political functions. I doubt whether the science of psychology was in a position to make a contribution of any value at the time when female suffrage was a subject of political conflict. The problem which had to be solved was determined by factors of a very different kind. Apart from the application of such political principles as that which regards the right of representation as a necessary result of taxation, the issue was largely determined by personal preferences and prejudices, and on grounds of political expediency, while perhaps the

13

most striking fact is that in our own country the final and peaceful outcome of the conflict was largely, if not mainly, determined by a purely affective state, viz. the gratitude of the community to women for all that they had done during the war. Moreover, while women were deprived of political functions there was no possibility of any real knowledge of their qualification for the art of government, except, of course, in so far as political power had been entrusted to them in connection with other bodies than parliament and in other countries. Whereas, after women have exercised political functions, the world comes into possession, or should come into possession, of a mass of facts which make scientific study possible. The point I wish to make is that the observation of the political behaviour of women, and of the differences, if there be such, between their political behaviour and that of men, is capable of supplying us with a mass of facts which make a real contribution to our knowledge of the psychology of the sexes ; which will tell us whether there are psychological differences and the nature of such differences, if they exist, between men and women. One kind of fact of which I am thinking would be derived from a study of the relative proportions of men and women who vote, and especially of any differences in this respect between local elections where the issues are readily appreciated as compared with parliamentary elections where the issues are more confused and intangible. Another kind of fact would be derived from the study of the nature of legislation before and after the introduction of female suffrage, especially in matters of education and hygiene. Especially valuable in this respect would be the evidence from regions so like one another as those of the United States of America at the time when only some of these states had adopted this form of suffrage. My point is that the observation and statistical study of political behaviour is capable of contributing far more to our psychological knowledge of any differences between the two sexes than such knowledge otherwise gained has been able to contribute towards the solution of the political problems involved.

Again, it will only be through the utilisation of facts of this kind combined with other lines of evidence that we can expect the solution of the far more difficult problem whether if differences in the political behaviour of men and women are shown to exist, they are inherent in the nature of the two sexes or are determined by the factors which Graham Wallas has summarised so aptly under the heading of social heritage. The point on which I wish to insist is that just as I have previously held that it is only through the comparative study of that special kind of behaviour we call warfare that we can expect to understand the place taken by the emotion of revenge in human history, so in politics it is only through the study of political behaviour that we can hope to understand the real nature of the psychological factors which enter into this behaviour. Both in the broader field of comparative sociology and in the narrower field of politics, knowledge of the facts of social and political behaviour can make a far greater contribution to our psychology than any psychological knowledge we possess at present can contribute to our understanding and treatment of social and political problems.

A striking example of the thesis I am putting forward is, in my opinion, provided by the great book of our Chairman on *Human Nature in Politics*. Throughout that book the author modestly implies that he is engaged in applying psychological knowledge to the elucidation of political behaviour. I venture to put forward the somewhat different view that the most important contribution made by that book is that it gave us a body of evidence collected by one who, while taking part in political life, had succeeded in keeping alive the capacity for dispassionate observation ; that, by the study of political behaviour, recorded in *Human Nature in Politics* Graham Wallas contributed far more to psychology than he was helped by it. It is true that through other lines of work the science of psychology was moving in the direction along which Graham Wallas was led by his political observations, but the special contribution of that book was its demonstration that the factors to which others were being led through the study of morbid states of the individual are also active in the collective behaviour of our own people in the political sphere.

I fear that what I have said in introducing the subject of the relation between psychology and politics may be disappointing to those who have been expecting that I should be able to point clearly to the value of psychological knowledge to the politician. I have deliberately chosen, however, to begin in this way because if there is any truth in what I have said the lesson to which it points is clear. The psychologist of politics cannot make bricks without straw. You cannot expect him to formulate laws concerning the motives of political behaviour unless he has the data whereon to found hypotheses and the facts wherewith to test those hypotheses.

If there is any truth in the view I have put before you, what is needed if we are to advance in knowledge is the collection of data derived from the observation of political behaviour, using the terms " observation " and " behaviour " in a very wide sense. These data fall into several classes of which two may be clearly distinguished from one another. One class of facts which should be available for the use of the psychologist are the records, usually more or less statistical in form, which are already collected by government departments or are capable of such collection. The other main class will be derived from the direct observation by those trained in psychology of the various forms of political behaviour, of which kind of observation I have already cited the work of Graham Wallas as an example. In considering these two forms of observation I will begin by stating my conviction not only that the second kind of observation is by far the more important of the two, but also that it is the more immediately necessary and that the knowledge derived therefrom is essential to the successful utilisation of statistical data. The social psychologist is here confronted with a problem very similar to that which was presented thirty years ago to the individual psychologist when he was first introduced to the experimental method. Carried away by the glamour and attractiveness of a new method, many believed that the problems of psychology were going to be solved by experimental methods. Advocates of what in those days was called the " new psychology " firmly believed that the more they refined their methods and measured by the thousandth of a second, and the more they multiplied the observations so made and applied to them the most elaborate statistical methods, the sooner they would reach the psychological millennium. The hopes thus raised have been rudely disappointed, though believers still linger here and there. The disillusionment came because the advocates of these new methods did not appreciate the fact that we need knowledge derived from the close qualitative study of the individual mind, and from the comparison of its nature under such variation of conditions as disease provides, before we can expect to be able to utilise such statistical data as are provided by the very limited forms of mental activity to which the experimental method is capable of application.

It is very necessary that the social psychologist should now avoid the similar danger into which he may fall. It is essential that he shall recognise that he will not be in a position to learn much from the psychological interpretation of social and political statistics until he has prepared the field by a close and immediate study of social and political behaviour. I propose to devote what remains of this lecture to a brief examination of two examples of political behaviour which need far closer study than they have hitherto received.

One of these is the behaviour of the committee which is so prominent in the mechanism of government; the other is the behaviour associated with bureaucracy.

The committee now occupies so important a position in our system of government; it is an instrument so obviously capable of being turned to good or evil purpose according to the way it is conducted, that it needs definite study of a kind which, so far as I know, has never been attempted. At the same time it is a study from which a successful issue can hardly be expected except on the basis of psychological knowledge and by the application of psychological method.

Committees are of many kinds and work with very different degrees of success. One important distinction which could be made is according to the nature of their functions, and especially whether they are advisory or have executive functions. My own impression, it is nothing more than an impression, is that the committees of the former kind, with which I am acquainted, are a success and those of the latter kind often a failure. It is evident that a form of grouping which is adapted to one kind of social or political function need not, and probably will not, be suitable for another, and the two kinds of function which differ from one another so greatly as those denoted by the terms " advisory " and " executive " would probably need instruments of different kinds. Committees might also be classed according to the nature of their mode of working and of their results. We probably all know the committee which does little more than support and register the decisions of one of its members, in which the result may be better or worse than that which would be reached by its members acting individually, according as the master mind is superior or inferior to the rest. Leaving this frequent case on one side, it will probably be widely recognised that some committees reach conclusions definitely superior to those which would be reached by their individual members, while other committees may produce results altogether on a lower level than the decisions of their constituent members if acting as individuals. Certain factors to which such differences may be due are fairly obvious. The former result is the more likely to be reached the more the individual members are able to contribute special knowledge, and are ready to put this knowledge in the possession of others. The latter result is the more likely when the members of the committee have not the adequate knowledge or, if they have it, have not the courage, the enterprise, sometimes perhaps the honesty, to put it forward, but allow the opinion of the more vocal members to carry the day. Here again I should like to register the impression that there is a tendency for this mode of classification of committees to coincide with that which distinguishes committees according to their advisory or executive functions, the advisory committee tending to produce a result superior to that which would be reached by its individual members, while the committee of the executive class is one in which the result often tends to be of a kind one has to regard as inferior to that of the individual members. I only put forward this suggestion in the most tentative manner, for I believe that the whole subject needs an exhaustive examination, through the results of which I believe it would be possible to reach conclusions which would make the committee an institution of greater value to the community, or at least reduce the magnitude of certain unsatisfactory aspects of this mode of government which cannot altogether be abolished.

The other subject to which I should like to refer briefly, though here again only by way of illustration of the kind of way in which psychology may be useful to politics, is one connected with what is usually called bureaucracy, a subject perhaps of as great and as immediate political importance as any other which can be named. There is no question that the greatest obstacle to the management of production, distribution and consumption in the interest of the community is the general dread of certain evils which have become closely connected in public opinion with government control, a dread which has been greatly accentuated by the experience of nearly everyone who had to do with government departments, at any rate with certain government departments, during the war. One of the most important problems with which our society is confronted is to discover how to administer and manage enterprises of various kinds without the evils which are summed up under the name bureaucracy. There can be little question that we have here a subject in which psychology can be of service. Here again we need an exhaustive study of the factors which enter into management, among which, of course, the subject with which I have just dealt, the committee, will rank as one of the most important. This is not the place, even had I the necessary knowledge, to enter upon the full consideration of this subject, but as an illustration of the kind of problem with which the investigating psychologist would have to deal I may mention the highly important and widespread social institution known as " red tape." It is obvious that in the conduct of any extensive business one cannot trust to the unregulated individual judgment of everyone concerned in management, but that there have to be definite rules of procedure. The state or process which is known as " red tape " is one in which these rules are unduly complex and unduly rigid, and have become masters instead of servants. Here again I shall make no attempt to deal with the subject fully, but shall be content to throw out a suggestion concerning one kind of psychological process which acts as a factor in the misuse of a necessary procedure.

Modern psychology is largely concerned with the mechanisms by which certain mental products, and especially those products we regard as morbid, come into being. Among the many processes or mechanisms it has distinguished is one which is called the defence-mechanism. A good example of this process is the exaggerated confidence, often amounting to bluster and swagger, which is adopted by those who, under the surface, have a definite sense of inferiority. I think that most educated people now recognise that many examples of exaggerated social behaviour only cover an attitude of self-distrust and doubt. The psychologist classes this mode of behaviour, with many others of different kinds, as due to the action of a defence-mechanism in which the blustering or swaggering attitude is adopted, not of set purpose, but more or less unwittingly, as a defence against the unpleasant state of mind which would be present if the inferiority were explicitly recognised. I should like to suggest that one of the factors which enters into the production of " red tape " is the activity of a defence-mechanism ; that it is a protection adopted in a more

24

or less, usually more rather than less, unwitting manner by those who find themselves confronted with administrative problems to which their powers are not adequate. My own experience of individual experts in the use of " red tape " certainly points in this direction, while it is significant that it flourishes luxuriantly in such departments as the War Office, where men who enter upon the career of arms because they have the qualifications for fighting and adventure find that their essential task is the management of a vast organisation in which the qualities especially needed are very different from those which led them to adopt the army as a career. I must be content to throw out this suggestion as to one of the lines which may serve as a guide in the psychological investigation of an attitude which must be understood if we are to correct the evils now associated with government control.

I must be content with these examples of the kind of way in which psychology may be able to help towards the solution of certain practical problems, but I should like to insist again that these must only be regarded as examples of the kind of problem to which psychological methods and principles may be applied. As a beginner in the study of politics it is not my place to attempt the practical application of psychology to such problems. I believe that any qualifications

25

I may have for dealing with the subject of this course of lectures will be better employed if I deal with some of the fundamental problems of social psychology, and in the next lecture I propose to take as my subject the importance of instinct in the study of the sociological problems of which political problems form so important a part.

INSTINCT IN RELATION TO SOCIETY

II

INSTINCT IN RELATION TO SOCIETY

FOR the purpose of this lecture I propose to define instinct very briefly as " inherited disposition to behaviour." In so far as the behaviour of a human being is determined by dispositions which he has brought into the world with him as part of his psychical and mental make-up, so far shall I regard this behaviour as instinctive, and in so far as it is determined by his experience in relation to his environment, so far shall I regard the behaviour as otherwise determined, or non-instinctive.

The usual contrast made is between instinctive and intelligent behaviour, but I have made no reference to intelligence in the preceding definition because I do not want to commit myself to the position that instinctive and intelligent behaviour are mutually exclusive. It seems possible, if not probable, that we shall find ourselves sooner or later driven to the position that intelligent behaviour, or, to use a more abstract term, intelligence, may, in some cases at any rate, be determined by inheritance, in which case we should have to classify instincts into intelligent and non-intelligent. It seems to me far more likely, however, that we shall not follow this course, but shall be driven to give up the whole attempt to distinguish between instinct and intelligence and shall adopt a new classification with a new nomenclature. In my book on *Instinct and the Unconscious* I have made a beginning in this direction, and have distinguished between protopathic and epicritic instincts or forms of instinctive behaviour, making the presence or absence of discrimination and gradation the distinguishing marks of the two. I am not absolutely wedded to these terms, which have been taken from the physiology of sensation, and am quite prepared to accept other terms or even other distinctions, if better can be found. The important point which has not yet, I think, been adequately realised by the critics of that book is that this new classification and nomenclature form only a first attempt to find a new principle of classification of mental states which involves giving up the old attempt to distinguish between instinct and intelligence. In the simple definition which I adopt for the purpose of this lecture, I make no attempt to define instinct by means of psychological characters as discovered by introspection. The definition turns wholly on the words " inherited " and " behaviour " and may be regarded as frankly biological in character.

Two points follow from this definition. One of these which is now, I think, clearly recognised by nearly all writers, if not by all writers on instinct, is that, whatever may be the case in such animals as insects, purely instinctive behaviour is almost unknown in the case of the higher animals, and especially in man. There is much reason to believe that it is only on the first occasion on which an example of innate behaviour occurs that it can be regarded as purely instinctive, and that directly this behaviour is modified by experience, even by the experience derived from the first performance, it is no longer purely instinctive. It might seem that such a view as this might lead us to reject the concept of instinct when dealing with man, and it may be that we may eventually be driven to adopt this course, but there is so much reason to believe that different forms of human behaviour depend in varying degrees on innate dispositions that we cannot ignore the factor of heredity. We cannot put on one side the fact that such forms of behaviour as flight from danger, or that actuated by the sexual impulse, belong to a category vastly different from the highly specialised and discriminative behaviour which has just led me to choose the word " impulse " in the

31

earlier part of this sentence, or that which each one of you is exemplifying when you come and listen to a lecture on psychology instead of going to a theatre or enjoying the comfort of your own homes. We are now inclined to believe that if such highly complex examples of behaviour as those I have just instanced were fully analysed we should come upon factors of the innate order which would therefore be included in our definition of instinct. But there is a vast difference between the crude and universal modes of behaviour connected with self-preservation and sex, and the highly specialised, individual, and exceptional behaviour of the kind I have exemplified by the choice of a word or the mode of spending an evening.

In what I have just said I have used a word which implies an important distinction which is often made between instinctive and non-instinctive behaviour. I have spoken of behaviour connected with self-preservation and sex as universal, and I wish now to consider how far universality can be taken as a distinguishing feature of instinct. In the case of the lower animals the statement that an instinct is of universal occurrence among all the members of the species may be taken as practically true, though exceptions or perversions certainly occur, and it is customary to apply the same distinction to the instincts of man. We can have no doubt that certain forms of behaviour for which we possess inherited dispositions, such as suckling, repulsion by the painful, and the primary impulses connected with sex are thus universal, though this universality may only be true of certain epochs of life, while, owing to the enormous extent to which the instincts of man are capable of modification, it may be obscured by the great variety of form which, through such modification, behaviour primarily instinctive may come to take. There are other cases in which the behaviour of different individuals or of different societies varies so greatly that it may not be easy to find any common feature which can be regarded as universal. But it is a question whether in many of these cases the universality has only been disguised by the high degree of modification of which human instincts are capable. Thus, observation of the behaviour of different members of our own community might lead us to doubt whether the disposition to flee from danger, with its accompanying affect of fear, is universal, and if we confine our attention to the healthy adult, we might well doubt whether this form of behaviour, generally assumed to be instinctive, is universal even in our own society, but the observation of the behaviour of the child and of the adult when affected by disease, or even of the normal adult when exposed to exceptionally

33

dangerous situations, provides conclusive evidence that this instinctive behaviour is universal and that the universality is only disguised by such processes as suppression and sublimination. Consequently, it is not necessary to give up universality within the species as a distinguishing mark of instinct in man.

There is, however, another possibility which may make it necessary to modify the current view that every member of a species exhibits the working of the instincts of that species. Not long ago it was generally assumed that hereditary characters only come into being through the agency of natural selection, and this view involves the consequence that instincts must be universal in the species. If, on the other hand, acquired characters can be transmitted, it becomes possible that the highly diverse varieties of mankind may have acquired different instincts. Largely owing to the discovery of the agencies called hormones, by which the activity of one part of the body influences others independently of the nervous system, the whole problem of the inheritance of acquired characters has again been brought into the field of possibility. If observation and experiment should prove the existence of this mode of heredity, it will open the field to the existence of instincts which are not universal to mankind but are confined to certain peoples or societies.

Moreover, this course of events will have as a consequence the situation that human instincts may vary from one another greatly in their degree of fixity, their inevitableness, and their modifiability. We should expect that such instincts as those of self-preservation and sex, which must go back very far in phylogenetic development, should be relatively fixed or capable only of modification through such deeply seated processes as suppression, while instinctive behaviour recently acquired would be capable of far more easy inhibition, or even of complete replacement by behaviour of a different kind. The different degrees of plasticity of instinct which would follow from the inheritance of acquired characters would have other consequences which would open many new problems.

It may perhaps surprise you that in a lecture on the relation between psychology and politics I am finding it necessary to wander into the field opened by the mere possibility of the occurrence of the inheritance of acquired characters, and at this point I may consider briefly just what makes this topic so important. I may illustrate by a problem which I have already considered briefly elsewhere.*

The comparative study of different human societies shows the presence of very striking

* See *Instinct and the Unconscious*, 2nd edition, 1922, page 260.

differences in relation to the attitude towards property. Some societies, of which our own is an example, have so strong a leaning towards individual ownership that their members often believe as an article of faith that common ownership is contrary to human nature, while other societies are so wedded to common ownership that they find it equally difficult to understand our individualism and may find it even as grotesque and ridiculous as many of the customs of savage peoples appear to us.

As an example I may cite an experience of my own which any of you who heard me read a paper last year at the Anthropological Club of this University will already know. When I was travelling in 1908 on a vessel with four Polynesian natives of Niue or Savage Island, and took the opportunity of inquiring into their social organisation, they retaliated in a manner I am always glad to encourage by asking me about the social customs of my own country. Using my own concrete method, one of the first questions was directed to discover what I should do with a sovereign if I was fortunate enough to earn one. In response to my somewhat lame answers, they asked me the definitely leading question whether I should share it with my parents, brothers and sisters. When I replied that I might do so if I liked, but that it was not the usual custom, they found my reply so ridiculous that it was long before they left off laughing. It was quite clear from their ejaculations that their amusement was altogether due to the incongruity with their own attitude of my conduct with regard to my earnings. Their attitude towards my individualism was of just the same kind as that which we experience when we hear of such a custom as the couvade or of many examples of sympathetic magic, and revealed the presence of a communistic sentiment of a deeply seated kind.

When, as among ourselves at the present moment, the student of politics is confronted with problems which largely depend on the nature of the attitude towards individual and common ownership, or towards individual and common management of property, the strength, and still more the permanence, of the sentiments upon which this attitude rests become of great importance. If we exclude the inheritance of acquired characters from the field, two chief possibilities remain as a means of explaining the different attitude towards property shown by the Polynesians and ourselves. One of these is that the attitude towards property has no instinctive basis, but is purely a matter of what Graham Wallas has called " social heritage " ; the other, that if there is an instinct underlying individual ownership, it is capable of being suppressed or sublimated through other agencies, of which presumably one of the most important is the gregarious instinct; or it may be the case that this suppression or sublimation is capable of being brought about through the agency of the traditional sentiments which make up so large a part of our social heritage. In either case there is no reason why one kind of attitude towards ownership should not be speedily converted into the other, and in the first case even in one generation. There is no reason why the Polynesian or the Melanesian should not speedily become a firm adherent of individual ownership, and equally no reason why we should not just as speedily acquire a sentiment in favour of common ownership.

If, on the other hand, the inheritance of acquired characters should make it possible that there have come into being instinctive attitudes towards property widely different from one another, we must expect that it will take longer to modify existing sentiments and that the reformer will have to trust far more to the agencies of suppression and sublimation.

In the preceding discussion of the universality and plasticity of instinct in its relation to politics, I have mentioned the gregarious instinct as one of the agencies by means of which an instinct prompting individual acquisition may have been inhibited and controlled. I propose to devote the greater part of this lecture to the consideration of this instinct, or group of instincts, now widely and popularly known as the herd-instinct.

In recent psychological literature we read far more about the activity and effects of the herd-instinct than about what this instinct is. Singularly few attempts have been made to justify the instinctive character of the processes by which the social group influences the individual, to distinguish between those elements which are instinctive and those which form part of the social heritage. The whole matter requires a prolonged and detailed study based upon evidence from many different fields ; from the comparative study of different human societies ; from the observation of the behaviour of the child ; from the study of disorders of the mental life due in the main to conflicts between individual tendencies and social or gregarious factors ; from that wider study in which human behaviour is regarded biologically in its relation to that of other animals ; while still another line of approach is to be found in the comparison of the behaviour of solitary and gregarious animals whether in a state of nature or under domestication, bearing in mind that when an animal is domesticated by man it becomes in a way a member of human society acting upon its members just as it is acted on by them.

Although little has yet been done towards

the distinction of the instinctive from the non-instinctive elements of the complex influence which the group exerts upon the individual, several attempts have been made to classify the processes included under the term " herd-instinct." Thus Trotter * has distinguished between offensive and defensive gregariousness, and he and many others have recognised the different nature of gregariousness in such animals as the wolf, the sheep and the bee. So far as I am aware, however, no writer has clearly distinguished between two varieties of gregariousness, the distinction and study of which are of the greatest importance, especially in relation to the instinctive aspect of man's social behaviour.

Two main varieties of gregarious group can be distinguished both in the lower animals and in man. In one the group has no definite leader. In the other there is not only such a leader, but the attitude towards him becomes a most important factor in the maintenance of social cohesion.

In many animal groups we can be confident that there is no one individual distinguished from the rest either by superior powers or superior equipment and the unity which characterises the behaviour of animal societies so composed must depend on some property by which each member of the group acts upon, or is capable of acting upon every

* *Instincts of the Herd in Peace and War*, 1920, page 28.

other member of the group with the high degree of uniformity necessary to ensure the harmony of this behaviour. In so far as the behaviour of such a society is instinctive it provides the simplest case of herd-instinct, and the process upon which the unity and harmony of action depend provides the prototype of the " suggestion " which I have used * as the term for the comprehensive process by means of which all the members of a group act with harmony towards some common end.

In another kind of group, which we must regard as more complex, behaviour is, or may be, of a character in which some one member of the herd takes a more prominent position than the rest. When this prominent position is always, or for prolonged periods, occupied by the same individual, we have a definite example of the second variety of gregariousness in which the group has a definite leader. It is probable that there are many intermediate varieties in which any member of the group is capable of acting as leader, chances of time and space determining which member shall be the leader at any given moment. How far this occasional leadership makes necessary differentiation within the group will depend on the nature of the functions connected with the position

* *Instinct and the Unconscious*, Cambridge University Press, 2nd edition, 1922, page 91.

of especial prominence, and we need far more extensive and exact observation of the behaviour of gregarious animals than we possess at present to allow any definite statements under this head.

When there is a definite leader, it is evident that the conditions determining the behaviour of the group will be vastly different from those of the leaderless group. In addition to the process of suggestion taking place in an equal degree and in a similar manner between every member of the group, or being at least capable of taking place between every member of the group, there is now a specialised form of the process between one member of the group and all its other individual members.

The process by which in this case the harmony of the group is ensured must be so different from that which is in action when there is no leader that the two forms of group and corresponding unifying processes must be clearly distinguished from one another and should receive different designations. The process by which the leader influences the group, and is doubtless influenced by its other members, may be regarded as the prototype of the process known as prestige-suggestion, the process which is so prominent in the suggestion of hypnotism, of the medical consulting-room, and of political leadership.

Before I pass on to consider how far these

two main varieties of the herd-instinct are represented in man and the part which it may be possible to assign to them in connection with politics, I must point out a most important distinction between them, one which involves factors of the utmost importance from the psychological point of view.

So long as the herd is leaderless and its harmony dependent on the reciprocal influence which every member of the group exerts indiscriminately on every other member, there will be no need for that discrimination of the features by which one member of the herd differs from another, nor for any individual graduation of action apart from any discrimination or graduation of which the activity of the herd as a whole is capable. There will be a tendency to behaviour of the all-or-none kind such as is exemplified in panic, or less completely in the apparently blind mimesis * which leads every member of a flock of sheep to follow the example set by any one of its members. The behaviour of the whole group will be, or tend to be, unwitting. There will be no opening for such differentiation of individual behaviour such as we must suppose to be connected with witting as distinguished from unwitting behaviour.

The greater variety of the conditions of the group with a leader not only makes it

* *Instinct and the Unconscious*, page 92.

43

more complex, but introduces the necessity of more complex behaviour. While each member maintains the relations with the rest of the group, which are necessary to ensure harmony of behaviour, there will now be added the attitude of each member towards the leader. It seems clear that a leader would be of little advantage to the group if the attitude towards him were not combined with those relations between the members of the group in general as were necessary to ensure the harmony of its action when there was no leader. If, for the present, we continue to call the general process by which the harmony of the leaderless herd is maintained " suggestion," and the process through which the leader exerts his influence " faith," the situation which I have just outlined in the case of the herd with a leader would involve the activity of both suggestion and faith while the harmony of the leaderless herd would require only the activity of the process of suggestion. The point, however, on which I desire now to lay stress is that the process of faith will be of a far more witting kind than the suggestion of the leaderless herd, involving as it does not only the discrimination of the leader from the rest of the herd, but also the discrimination of the nature of his behaviour with its corresponding graduation of conduct, though the greater the degree of organisation of the leadership, the less witting would the discrimination and graduation become.

At this stage it will be convenient to stay for a moment to consider a problem of nomenclature. If the foregoing sketch is valid, it will be necessary to distinguish very definitely between the nature of the processes of the herd with and without a leader. I have elsewhere * analysed the general process of suggestion, and have distinguished sympathy, mimesis, and intuition as its component elements according as we are concerned with the affective, conative or cognitive aspects of the process. It is clear that a similar analysis should be carried out in the case of the process of the group with a leader.

Beginning with the affective aspect it is clear that something more is involved in the attitude towards the leader than sympathy, and that there is, at least, the root of the process we call reverence. In the attitude of each member of a herd towards its leader I see as its essential element the process which gives to reverence its distinguishing character.

On the conative side again it is clear that we have something more than the blind mimesis of the leaderless group. The members of the group do not merely imitate

* *Instinct and the Unconscious*, page 90.

45

the motions of the leader, but in all but the simplest cases their ways of reacting to his gestures are more varied and complex. The attitude of activity towards the leader has in it as its essential element the factor which is also at the root of obedience, and for the present I should like to propose obedience as a term for the conative aspect of the process by which the behaviour of the members of the group towards the leader is regulated. They do not imitate but they obey.

Here, as in the case of the processes of the leaderless group, it is in connection with the cognitive aspect of the process that the chief difficulty in nomenclature arises. It is clear that in the group with a leader there will be something more than the unwitting intuition by which each member of the group responds to the activity of every other member. As, in my opinion, we have here the root of the process of cognition (and, as I believe, the process to be essentially that which we understand by cognition), I shall be content for the present to use this term, and when it is necessary I should speak of the cognitive aspect of the attitude towards the leader. The important point to recognise now is that in the attitude towards the leader of the group we have the germ, if not the essence, of the processes we call faith, reverence and obedience, and that these processes are not present in the

46

more unwitting behaviour of the leaderless group.

I cannot stay here to develop further these differences between the behaviour and processes which characterise the activity of the group with and without a leader, but must pass on to consider, it can be only briefly, how far we can distinguish the presence of these two varieties of group-behaviour in man and how far the study of early forms of the social group helps us to understand the nature of the social activity of man. I have considered elsewhere * certain lines of evidence which point to the existence in man of behaviour characterised by an unwitting activity of the processes of the sympathy, mimesis and intuition which I regard as the distinguishing marks of the behaviour of the leaderless herd, and I propose to-day to confine my attention to the nature of the attitude towards the leader of a human group.

In discussing how far it is possible to get back to the roots of the attitude of the human group towards its leader, it is of the first importance to know what was the nature of the social group among the progenitors of man. As you are probably aware, we here strike upon one of the most disputed and disputable problems of anthropology. According to one view the earliest human group corresponded closely with that formed by

* *Instinct and the Unconscious*, page 94.

the modern family; according to another it resembled rather the clan of many existing simple societies with a far-reaching system of communism among its members; while according to a third point of view the earliest human group differed from any at present in existence in being composed of a sire with many wives, for the mastery of whom the sons strove when the sire died or became unable to maintain his exclusive rights over the women of the group. I have no intention of attempting any survey of the anthropological evidence for or against these different views. I must be content to say that in my opinion this evidence points to the communistic clan as a group which was not the original unit of human society but one which only came into existence under certain conditions, and especially the development of agriculture, which enabled men to live in larger groups than that formed by the family. Perhaps it has not even been universal among mankind. There is much reason to believe that the early form of human grouping was small. At a time when men lived by the collection of berries, nuts, roots, grubs and small game, they could hardly have existed except under conditions where a territory of considerable size was necessary to satisfy the appetite of each individual and a group of considerable size would have been impossible. At the present time the Australian aboriginal forms our best example of a people in the collecting stage, and it is said that in some parts of Australia a man may have to travel forty miles a day to get his daily food. Under such circumstances, or even in more luxuriant countries, the existence of a large human group would be impossible, and we may conclude with some certainty that the early human group consisted of little more than parents and children forming a family group either of the modern form or of the polygynous kind, the nature of which I have briefly indicated.

If the early human group was of this kind the leader was also the father, and if there is in mankind an instinctive attitude towards the leader it will have been complicated in its development by the inclusion of elements arising out of the attitude towards the father. Moreover, if the early group was of the polygynous kind, with a monopoly of all the women of the group by the leader, there will have been introduced into the attitude towards the man who was both father and leader the element of jealousy, or even hatred, which the experience of the psycho-analyst leads him to look upon as a feature of the infantile attitude towards the father. We are here brought up against the important problem of modern psychology, usually connected with the term " Œdipus complex," but with the important element, not usually taken into account, that the special features of the attitude towards the father may not arise so much out of the actual relations of the modern family, but may be of an instinctive kind going back to features of an early form of social grouping.

I have led you to this topic with its highly disputable character because I believe that it furnishes a good example of the general principle to which I devoted the last lecture. It is unlikely that we shall ever obtain any direct evidence concerning the exact nature of the earliest form of human social grouping, while it is probable that, at any rate for a long time to come, it will be very difficult to estimate at its proper value the evidence reached by psycho-analytic inquiry. Neither anthropology nor psychology is likely to make conclusive contributions towards our understanding of the nature of leadership in the modern forms of social grouping. Just as we need close psychological study of such forms of social grouping as the Committee and the Government Department, so do we need a similar study of the attitude towards the modern social or political leader. Such a study is necessary if we are to find an answer to the many questions suggested by the nature of leadership in the modern state.

I propose now to proceed on the lines of my first lecture and consider briefly one or two examples of the questions which thus need an answer, not with the intention of attempting such an answer, but rather to state the kind of problem to the solution of which I hope some day psychology may be able to contribute. One of these problems concerns the nature of the process by which ideas influence human progress. One of the chief conclusions to which modern psychology is leading is that human behaviour is much less influenced by ideas than was formerly supposed, but responds rather to appeals made in the symbolic manner by which the subconscious or unconscious levels of the mind seem to be so greatly influenced. This kind of mechanism seems to leave but little scope for the motive power which has hitherto been universally ascribed to the great ideas of the world's history, to such ideas as underlay, or seem to have underlain, the Reformation and the rebellion against the autocracy of the Stuarts, or such ideas as the " Peace with Honour " or " Peace, Retrenchment and Reform " of the two great political parties of the latter part of the last century. The problem which I wish to raise concerns the part taken in the efficacy of these ideas by the personalities with whom they were associated. What was the part taken in the success of the ideas which seemed to actuate the Reformation by such personalities as that of Luther ; of the ideas of our own revolution by Hampden and Cromwell ; of " Peace with Honour " by the personality of Beaconsfield, of " Peace, Retrenchment and Reform " by Gladstone, and of the idea of " Tariff Reform " by Chamberlain ? The ease with which forms of words which once had a real meaning continue to be used in spite of the fact that they have degenerated into shibboleths and catchwords suggests an interesting psychological problem in which the process of symbolism certainly takes its part. It suggests that while the ideas are really active there is something more behind them than an appeal to intelligence, and that they owe much of their efficacy to the power of personality, possibly to the instinctive desire of the human group to have a leader to whom it can look for guidance in the same unwitting manner with which the members of a herd of animals regard their leader. The intervention of a long period in our own history in which the place of the leader has been taken by a king introduces a complicating factor into the psychological situation, a factor the importance of which is indicated by the frequent experience of psycho-analytic investigation in which the king acts as the surrogate of the father, while the corresponding place of the father or ideal leader in a country without a king may be taken by President, Governor or Mayor.

Examples of government in communistic communities, such as those of Melanesia, suggest that the leader is not essential to success in many lines of activity in which we are inclined to look upon him as indispensable. One of the most important, but at the same time most difficult problems now facing peoples moving towards, or striving to move towards, a genuine democracy is how far it will be possible for the immense communities of modern times to reach the harmony of social action which has been attained by many small communities without a leader or with a leadership the importance of which in social life has been reduced to very small dimensions. This is, however, looking far into the future. At present it seems fairly clear that no great movement is likely to succeed except under the leadership of one who is able to inspire a degree of confidence comparable with that which actuates the instinctive attitude of the animal herd towards its leader. If this be so, this conclusion has as its corollary the necessity of a personality which appeals more largely to the emotions than to the intelligence. Depressing as this conclusion may seem, I believe that no leader is likely to have a deep or permanent influence unless among those characters which appeal to the emotions of the group, and I hope as chief among them are to be found honesty and steadfastness of purpose and those altruistic sentiments which have been developed on the foundation of the common interests of which the herd-instinct is the deepest and oldest expression.

THE CONCEPT OF THE MORBID
IN SOCIOLOGY

III

IN works on sociology and politics it is a commonplace to use language derived from medicine when the writers are referring to features of society which are regarded as abnormal. When Mr Tawney, wishing to emphasise the unsatisfactory aspects of the social conditions of our civilisation, speaks of " the Sickness of an Acquisitive Society," or when we speak of the paralysis of a social institution or the convulsions of a revolution, we are using similes derived more or less directly from pathological states of the individual to denote states of society. In general such usage is only regarded as metaphorical, and so long as there is nothing more than an employment of metaphor and simile, no problem of importance is raised. I propose in this lecture, however, to deal with the question whether it may not be possible to use such terms in more than a metaphorical sense so that the words will carry over into their new application a significance definitely connected with that which they bear when they are used of the individual. The problem I wish to raise in this lecture is whether it is possible to use some part, at any rate, of the terminology of the medicine of the individual for the description and classification of states of society and for the methods by which these states may, when necessary, be treated by the statesman and social reformer. The problem before us will be whether it is possible, and if so whether it is expedient, to introduce into the science of sociology the concepts and terminology of disease.

Before I enter upon this topic one or two preliminary problems will have to be considered, and I will begin with one which has long aroused interest, viz. the question whether there is any utility in the analogy, or possibly more than the analogy, of society with the living organism. I do not believe that it is likely to be useful to introduce concepts and terminology derived from medicine into sociology and politics unless this analogy, or more than analogy, holds good.

The resemblance between society and the living organism is one which has long excited interest and has been frequently discussed, usually with results tending to belittle the value of the resemblance from the scientific point of view. The most recent discussion of the problem with which I am acquainted is that which we owe to Dr Morris Ginsberg, who has considered the matter in his valuable little book on *The Psychology of Society*. It would take up too large a part of this lecture to deal fully with his grounds for the rejection of the value of the analogy, and I can only consider them briefly.

Mr Ginsberg's first objection is that the analogy leads people to exaggerate the unity of society. To this I should answer that the modern conception of the organism, and especially of the human organism, is that it has much less unity and harmony than was once supposed. To speak at first on the purely physiological plane we know that the living body is the seat of conflicts between forces of many different kinds ; that various secretions of the body have actions antagonistic to one another, and that the apparent harmony of the body is due to a highly delicate process of adjustment whereby a balance is held between these conflicting forces. One of the chief conditions of the states we call disease is a breaking down of this balance and adjustment.

Again, we know that the body is the seat of a continuous conflict between certain intrinsic forces and external enemies in the forms of lowly organisms which are continually finding their way into the body in a manner closely comparable with the invasion of foreign enemies. We also know that there exist within the body countless hosts of other lowly organisms of a friendly sort, such as the

59

flora of the alimentary canal, upon whose peaceful collaboration the harmonious, or in other words, the healthy working of the organism largely depends. Even keeping in the region of pure physiology, and leaving the nervous system and the mind on one side, I am not sure that one who appreciates the vast complexity of the forces normally in conflict within the organism might not reverse Mr Ginsberg's objection and reject the analogy because it might lead us to exaggerate the unity of the living organism.

Mr Ginsberg's second objection is that the social community is infinitely complex, consisting of unity within unity, group within group. This has perhaps been already partially answered when dealing with the organism without mentioning the nervous system, but the objection becomes even less valid when the nervous system is taken into account, for this directive and regulative department of the living organism might with our present knowledge be described almost in Mr Ginsberg's words as consisting of unity within unity, group within group, the integration of which into a harmonious system is the function of its highest regions.

The third objection made by Mr Ginsberg, that the organic theory ignores the elements of conflict and disharmony which abound in the social community, has again, I hope, been already answered. I cannot refrain, however, from pointing out that when Mr Ginsberg goes on to say that the unity of society is not attained by the liberation of living energy but is only won by mechanical suppression and repression, he is even using the actual nomenclature by means of which we are now accustomed to describe the mechanisms by means of which the harmony of the living organism is attained in so far as this harmony is influenced by factors of a psychological kind.

A last objection made by Mr Ginsberg is one with which I have much sympathy, though it is of a practical kind rather than one inherent in the nature of the resemblance. Mr Ginsberg points out, I believe with justice, that the analogy between society and organism may tend to obscure the uniqueness of the position of the individual within the social organism, with the possible practical consequence that a belief in the unity of the social group may tend to weaken the sense of individual responsibility which every member of the group should possess. This practical difficulty, however, cannot be allowed to interfere with the concept of similarity of constitution if, on other grounds, this can be shown to exist.

I must be content for the present with this cursory reply to the most recent objections which have been made to the validity of the analogy between human society and the living organisms which form the individual elements of that society. It must be enough to say that modern knowledge concerning the living organism, both on the physiological and the psychological sides, teaches us that there is much less difference in complexity between society and organism than was formerly supposed, and that the difference between them is rather to be sought in the degree of plasticity and capacity for modification. Consequently, the difference between society and organism appears unduly great when we compare the living organism with a society like our own. It becomes far closer when we are dealing with those more lowly societies which, through long absence of the disturbing factors introduced by foreign influence, have become relatively stable and more fully adapted to their environment. The problems raised by the study of the many points of resemblance between society and organism will only become capable of solution when we have a far more extensive knowledge than we now possess of these two products of vital activity. For the present I am inclined to believe that the resemblance not only forms a useful guide to practice, but that we shall in time come to see that the resemblance is something more than an analogy, and depends on the operation of some fundamental laws of development common to both organism and society.

THE MORBID IN SOCIOLOGY

Among the many lines of approach to the establishment or disproof of such community of nature I believe that a foremost place will be taken by the study of the morbid states of each. If it should be possible to trace in the morbid states of both society and organism the action of certain common laws, and on the practical side to treat with success the morbid states of one by measures derived from the study of the other, we shall be forging links of a most important kind in the chain by which society and organism may be brought under one law or set of laws. Returning to the thesis of my first lecture, I must point out that the time is not yet ripe for the direct application of methods derived from the medicine of the individual to the morbid states of society, but rather that the resemblance between the two may provide us with a working scheme which must be tested by long and patient observation. There is little question that, backward as it may be, the medicine of the organism is more advanced than the medicine of society. While the one is now founded on definite principles and laws, the other is still in the stage of pure empiricism. Nevertheless it would be dangerous to apply the medicine of the individual to the disorders of society until we know far more than at present of the laws which regulate the normal working of society. At the same time I believe that the statesman and the politician would be largely assisted in obtaining this knowledge by the lessons to be learnt from the discipline which has as its subject the morbid state of the individual, and in this lecture I propose to consider as fully as time allows some points of resemblance between organism and society from the pathological standpoint.

I will begin by pointing out certain general resemblances between the general methods of medicine and those by which we must approach the evils of society. When a physician is called upon to treat the morbid state of an individual the first process he employs is diagnosis. Only when he has made up his mind as to the exact nature of the complaint is he in a position to undertake the proper treatment. Often he has to begin to treat his patient before he has finished his diagnosis, and then has to adopt palliative measures directed to relieve the immediate and often superficial symptoms, and when a complete diagnosis is impossible his treatment is never more than of this kind. But the essential feature of modern medicine is that the physician is not content, or should not be content, to treat symptoms, but bases his treatment upon a knowledge of the deeper morbid states of which the symptoms are but the superficial manifestation. The measures which follow the complete diagnosis are directed to restore to their normal state, as far as possible, the processes which have fallen into disorder. It is hardly necessary to point out how exactly this applies to the morbid states of society. Every student of political science recognises the necessity of going beneath the surface and seeking out the deeper and less obvious causes of social evils, but in practice the politician is just as prone to adopt the easy course of treating symptoms as is the unskilful or unscrupulous physician.

Another point of close resemblance between the morbid states of society and organism is the great difficulty and relative uncertainty of the prognosis in both. By prognosis in medicine we mean the process of foretelling the future course of the disease, and the great difficulty of this in each of the departments of life we are comparing is a necessary result of the immense complexity of the structures concerned. In this connection it may be noted that the greater the plasticity of the structure concerned, the greater will be the difficulty of prognosis, and that consequently it is, and will be, even with greater knowledge, more difficult to foresee the results of our political remedies than of those measures by which the physician treats the morbid states of the individual.

It will perhaps have appeared strange to some of you that in a course of lectures devoted to the relations between psychology and politics I should have devoted so much time to points of resemblance between the general principles of medicine and those by the application of which we may hope to remedy the evils of society. I have done so because this course is essential to the understanding of the modern attitude towards the morbid states of the individual mind in which we should expect to find the resemblance with the morbid states of society especially close. If I were asked to state the most important feature of the psychological medicine of to-day I should stress its adoption of the fundamental principle of the medicine of the body that we must not be content to treat the superficial symptom, but must get down to the roots of the mental malady. The older methods of hypnotism and suggestion, which not long ago dominated the medicine of the mind and are still so popular among the general public as well as among the less instructed of the medical profession, attempt nothing more than the treatment of symptoms. They make no attempt to reach the deeper causes to which these superficial manifestations are due. In the newer methods, on the other hand, the necessity is recognised of going to the roots of the malady, which is now one of the commonplaces of general medicine. At the present moment these new methods, sound as they are in principle, are in danger of falling into serious discredit through the vagaries and extravagances of those who are putting them into practice, but some of the lessons of the new psychiatry are so obvious that their value is coming to be recognised by all. I propose to deal with one or two of these well-established lessons and inquire whether they can help us in the diagnosis and treatment of the evils of society.

One of the most striking of these lessons of the new psychiatry teaches us the evil effects of repression, meaning by this term the process of putting unpleasant experience aside so that it may be forgotten, instead of facing the situation and tracing it to its sources so that it may be understood and suitable measures taken to put the situation right. There is an overwhelming mass of evidence to the effect that repression does not remove the evil, but that at the best the repressed experience remains in existence, always liable to flare up into activity later in life, while in the less favourable cases it leads directly to a whole series of morbid symptoms which greatly lower vitality and efficiency.

It is perhaps a significant fact that the word which has been chosen by the physician to designate this far-reaching morbid process of the individual life is one with which we are familiar when speaking of political activity. Before I proceed to compare the repression of psychological medicine with the repressive measures of politics, it will be well that we shall not trust to the mere resemblance of nomenclature, but shall begin by inquiring whether the repression of the physician is a process of the same order as the repression of the statesman or politician. In order to do so adequately it will be necessary to say that in my belief the repression of the psychiatrist is a term which includes in its denotation several processes which should be distinguished from one another. One distinction of great importance is the extent to which the process is put into action consciously, or, as I prefer to say, wittingly. We need far more study than has been given to the subject at present to enable us to understand the influence of different degrees of the witting application of repression, but it is evident that exactly the same kind of distinction holds good of social repression. In this case it is easy to recognise two very different varieties of the process. We all know the process by which a whole nation, or more frequently a whole class, shut out of their minds, apparently with success, whole regions of the social activities which are going on around them. How many are there who lead their lives without ever giving a thought to the poverty which appals those from the new countries of the world who visit this island, how many who never give a thought to the problems of the slums which perhaps lie within a stone's-throw of their luxurious homes. In this case the repression may be largely unwitting. The thought-process spontaneously avoids subjects which would arouse unpleasant states of mind. There may be no deliberate and witting turning of the attention from these to topics of a more agreeable kind, and the process is assisted in many cases by definite defence-mechanisms of which a good example is the well-established convention of polite society according to which it is bad form to make unpleasant social matters the subject of conversation. Far different from this is that process of repression by which a dominant class deliberately and wittingly represses all outward manifestations of the discontent which social wrongs arouse.

There is a close resemblance between the first of these two kinds of social repression and the individual process by which we unwittingly forget an obligation which would bring some unpleasant matter to consciousness. The similarity between this social process of repression and the process of purposive forgetting, the knowledge of which we owe so largely to Freud, is so close as to leave little doubt that we are dealing with one and the same process put into activity in the one case by an individual and in the other by a group. We are in a more difficult position when we turn to the second kind of more witting repression and consider whether there is any real community of nature between the process by which the individual thrusts unpleasant topics aside, and deliberately refuses to allow his mind to dwell upon them, and the equally witting process by which the leaders of a class prevent unpleasant topics from reaching those who might thereby become dissatisfied with the existing social order.

Before considering this matter I should like to point out a possible source of error derived from nomenclature. A large part of Freud's scheme of the psychology of the individual is based on his concept of the censorship, in which case he has employed a term derived from a purely social procedure to denote processes of the individual mind. Elsewhere * I have sought to show that this concept is of little, if any, value in helping us to understand the nature of individual mental process, and I now urge the further objection that by the application in individual psychology of a concept which has been definitely drawn from a social procedure Freud runs the danger of prejudicing the study of the relation between individual and social processes. The use of this term and concept implies a community of nature

---

* *Instinct and the Unconscious*, 2nd edition, 1922, page 228; *British Journal of Psychology* (General Lecture), 1921, vol. xii. page 113.

between individual and social process which can only be established by means of a far wider study than has yet been attempted. It is exceptional to find people who are not liable to be misled by verbal resemblances, and in comparing individual with social repression we must beware of being influenced by considerations based on the Freudian use of the concept of censorship.

Even apart, however, from the similarity between the individual and social processes of repression which suggested to Freud his use of the concept of the censorship, the witting repression of the individual and that of the group have much in common. It is now widely recognised that by repressing experience so that it no longer comes naturally to consciousness, the repressed experience is not thereby abolished, but persists below the surface and may manifest its presence in many indirect ways. According to the prevailing theory of the psycho-neuroses many of the symptoms of these disorders are the direct effect of the activity of such repressed or suppressed experience. Similarly, few can doubt that by the process of social repression the evils whose manifest expression is prevented do not thereby cease to exist, but smoulder on beneath the surface to break out into renewed activity when it is no longer possible to bear them in silence. In the individual it is now generally recognised that one of the most

71

frequent ways in which repressed or suppressed experience manifests itself is in the nightmare, in which the emotional state natural to the experience which has been repressed bursts out with an intensity far greater than that which would have accompanied its unrestricted expression in the waking life. Elsewhere * I have suggested that the social counterpart of the nightmare is the revolution ; that if the affects natural to the experience of social wrongs are not allowed to find expression in such a way as will lead to the recognition of the wrongs and to the measures which follow upon this recognition, there will sooner or later be violent and unregulated, all-or-none manifestations comparable with those of the nightmare.

The resemblances between the effects of individual and social repression are definitely reinforced when we turn to the nature of the treatment by which the morbid states may be remedied. The evidence is now conclusive that the occurrence of nightmares and other morbid states which follow upon repression in the individual disappear when the sufferer no longer attempts to put his troubles out of sight, but faces them and succeeds in dealing with them as if they had a less painful character. Especially important is it that he shall come to understand the nature of his

* *Dreams and Primitive Culture*, Manchester University Press, 1917-18, page 20.

troubles and shall appreciate the real reason, often very different from the apparent reason, why the experience which he has been repressing has gained its highly painful character. In other words the two requisites for the proper treatment of the states produced in the individual by repression are courage and knowledge ; courage to face experience from which there is a natural tendency to flee, as well as the still greater courage required to look closely into the nature of the painful experience and thus gain the knowledge which forms the other requisite for successful treatment. There can be little doubt that a similar process is necessary in the treatment of the social evils produced by repression or for which repressive measures have been employed by unwise rulers. Few who are capable of regarding social situations dispassionately can doubt the value of knowledge of the social evils in connection with which a crude policy of repression has been adopted. Here again the two things needed are courage and knowledge. Not only is the courage needed to face the social evils for which repression is usually employed of the same order as that needed by the individual when he is advised to face and understand the troubles he has been repressing. The knowledge needed is also of the same order, for in the social as in the individual case nothing is more valuable than the study of the process,

73

the historical process, by which the evils
have come into existence. In each case the
most important factor in treatment is the
discovery, and still more difficult, the acknow-
ledgment, of the faults by which the disorder
has been produced or accentuated.

I must be content this evening with this
brief comparison of the nature of repression
in the individual and in the group and of
the treatment by which the disorders following upon repression may be remedied.

Another example of the similarity in nature
and treatment between individual and social
disorders is to be found in connection with the
abuse of alcohol. In this case the resemblance between the intemperance of the individual and the intemperance of the group is so
obvious that there is no need to dwell upon it.
It will only be necessary to deal with certain
striking resemblances in the treatment of the
two kinds of disorder. Our new psychological
knowledge has had a great effect on the modern
treatment of alcoholism in the individual. In
the older modes of treatment the chief remedy
was removal for prolonged periods from the
temptations caused by ready access to the
means of obtaining alcohol, combined with
appeals to reason, based largely on moral
considerations. In some cases where it was
only necessary to break a morbid habit,
these lines of treatment were efficacious, but
failures were numerous. Modern methods of

treatment are based on the view that in many cases alcoholism is only a means of escape from some situation which the sufferer is unable to endure without the assistance provided by the lowering of sensibility and diminished powers of appreciation produced by alcohol. In other words resort to alcohol in such cases is a substitute for repression, or perhaps more correctly, it is a process by which a state allied to repression is produced by artificial means. The treatment now adopted is on the same lines as that for repression. The sufferer is taught to face his trouble, probe it to its source, and discover how it may be possible to live with it in peace so that it will be no longer necessary to have recourse to the paralysing agency of alcohol.

If there is any value in the resemblance between the morbid processes of the individual and of the group it seems fairly obvious that prohibition is a measure of the same order as the isolation and removal from temptation of the older way of treating the alcoholism of the individual. It is a characteristic example of the old method in which the physician was content to treat symptoms without discovering the real nature of the underlying morbid state which leads to the abuse of alcohol. The other old method of treating the individual by means of appeal to reason and moral considerations has also been applied in full force to the social evil,

75

but with little effect on the drink bill of the nation. It becomes a question whether the social malady should not be treated on lines comparable with those which are now being employed to combat the individual disorder, and whether we should not inquire far more insistently than at present into the deeper causes of the social evil. Here it would be well to have more knowledge comparable with that upon which the physician relies in his treatment of the individual. One example of such knowledge which the social reformer would like to possess is whether there is evidence for a relation between the prevalence of drunkenness and insufficient or inadequate housing. I was once told by a large owner of property of the striking influence in this respect produced in his experience by an extensive reconstruction of a town in which slums were abolished, and it ought to be possible to obtain records bearing on this relation. Even in the absence of such records I have little doubt that decent housing throughout the country would do much to remedy the more crying evils due to alcohol.

In stating this belief founded upon the application of the principles of the medicine of the individual to the medicine of society, I have perhaps gone beyond the task I set myself in the first lecture of stating problems rather than attempting their solution. Such conclusions as I have suggested are only, however, the outcome of the adoption of a principle in which modern knowledge only reinforces the teachings of common-sense, to the effect that in the society as with the individual we should not be content to treat symptoms, but should attack the deeper foundations upon which the symptoms rest.

I believe that here, as in the treatment of the social evils of alcoholism and repression, the suggestions derived from the medicine of the individual are so closely in accordance with reason and common-sense that we are even now justified in using them in many cases as guides, but this possibility of immediate practical application should not blind us to the fact that our treatment is experimental, and that measures should be employed in such a manner that their results may be tested and utilised as means of adding to that knowledge of social psychology whereby the principles there found useful may receive a more extended application. Every case in which we are able to demonstrate the value of the knowledge derived from the medicine of the individual in the treatment of social evils adds another link in the chain of evidence in favour of the view that the relation between society and organism is not merely a pleasing analogy, but has reference to an underlying community of nature.

I should like to conclude with a suggestion which will serve to bring the subject of this lecture into relation with that of last week. The main lesson to be drawn from the considerations laid before you this evening is that the principle of treating disorders of the individual mind by attacking underlying causes rather than superficial symptoms, which is the key-note of modern psycho-therapy, also holds good of social therapy.　Just as the physician is not now content to employ the agencies of faith and suggestion, whether used wittingly or unwittingly, but tries to lead his patient to a full understanding of his malady and of the causes by which it has been produced, and just as he attempts to bring about a relation between himself and his patient in which they work together with understanding towards a common end, so should it be with the social leader.　Whether it be in the smaller field of the group constituted by the family, the larger group formed by the school or college, or the still larger group formed by the nation, the leader should be one who is not satisfied to impose his will upon the group by the power of his personality and position, relying in the main upon the agencies of suggestion and faith, but should be one who takes the group into his confidence, leads them to see and understand what is amiss when evil conditions need to be remedied, and seeks to bring leader and led into a relation in which they work together with a common understanding towards a common goal.　At the present time, whether it be family, school or larger social group which is concerned, we have brought over into human leadership far too much of the crude attitude of the instinctive kind which we have inherited from our animal ancestry. But the collaboration of leader and led at which we should aim is not to be reached without far more understanding of the complex conditions of our society than exists at present. It is futile to speak of collaboration between leader and led in the modern state if the ideal of education is merely to train individual members of society to earn their bread in the existing industrial competition, and if a large part of the nation has not even the opportunity of obtaining the instruments by which the necessary knowledge may be acquired. If I am right in believing that the repair of social evils is to be effected on lines similar to those by which we are now learning to repair the disorders of the individual life, the chief immediate lesson is that we must not only make education readily accessible to every member of the community capable of benefiting by it. Quite as important, we must think far more seriously, and turn the best minds of the nation to the thought, of making education a means whereby the group may enter into that collaboration with its leaders so that the disorders of our civilisation may be remedied and the nation set upon a road which will lead it back to health and sanity.

When I set out to put together some views concerning the relation between psychology and politics I had no idea where I should be led. I had no idea that the two topics of leadership in its relation to the herd-instinct which was the subject of my last lecture and the study of the resemblance between society and organism with which I have dealt to-night would lead me, in what I hope has been strict logical sequence, to the crying need for education and for the reform of education in which our chairman of this evening has so great an interest and for which he has done and is doing so much.

AN ADDRESS ON SOCIALISM
AND HUMAN NATURE

IV

I IMAGINE that I have been asked to speak on the subject of " Socialism and Human Nature " in the hope that I may be able to throw some light by means of psychological and anthropological knowledge upon the statement so frequently heard that socialism is contrary to human nature. According to those who make this statement the habits of individualism and competition are so deeply engrained in human nature that the co-operation in the interest of the community which is the essential process underlying socialism has no chance of fruition.

Owing to the shortness of the time at my disposal I do not propose to take up your time with any attempt to define socialism. It must be sufficient to say that when I speak of socialism I mean a form of society the individual members of which are ready to work for the common good without the

* An address given to The Critical Society at University College on 25th May 1922.

incentive that they as individuals are going to reap an immediate advantage from their labour. If I had had time I should have liked to give you definite examples of such societies and of social practices which would come within this meaning of socialism. I must be content with one example. In Melanesia all the members of a social group of considerable size are allowed the use of the produce of the cultivated land of the group regardless whether they have taken any part in the cultivation or have contributed in any other manner to produce the commodities needed by the group. This is, of course, an extreme case, but it illustrates how fully such communities are imbued with concepts and sentiments connected with common property.

In order to save time I propose for the moment to say no more about what I mean by socialism. I must ask you to accept the fact of its existence in the simple societies of many parts of the earth. I wish to-day to inquire rather into what is meant when it is said that this form of society is " contrary to human nature."

Probably most of those who use these words have never thought what they mean but repeat them as a well-sounding expression by means of which they can dispose of what is to them an unpleasant subject about which they do not wish to think. Those

who are not content with this easy course
would like to know whether it is meant
that there is something in the innate constitution of the human mind which makes it
impossible for the members of a group to
collaborate in the interests of the group
or whether it is only meant that human societies have come into the possession of traditions
which inculcate individualistic sentiments and
practices. According to this second view
the individualism of our own society would
form part of what Graham Wallas has called
our social heritage as opposed to something
inherent in the constitution of the human
mind. If this second point of view be that
chosen by the adherents of the view that
socialism is contrary to human nature, it
would follow that we have only to change
the nature of the social environment and
human nature would change in a corresponding manner. There would be no reason
why even in a generation the Melanesian
should not become as good an individualist
as any member of the Conservative or Liberal
parties, or why we, also in one generation,
should not become as good socialists as the
Melanesian. I assume, therefore, that when
anyone says that socialism is contrary to
human nature he means that there is some
innate disposition of the human mind which
is incompatible with this form of society.
Such an innate disposition is what the psycho-

logist calls an instinct, so that the meaning we must ascribe to our phrase is that man possesses an instinct or group of instincts which makes it impossible for the individual to act for the common good unless he or she is aware that the action for the common good will also be for his or her individual good. Since the aspect of socialism which attracts most interest is that connected with property and the management of property, the instinct involved in this case will be the instinct of acquisition, and the first step in the process of discovering whether from this point of view socialism is contrary to human nature would be to discover whether such an instinct of acquisition exists. I have already considered this matter elsewhere * and have come to the conclusion that man possesses an instinct prompting him to acquisition in the interest of the individual. If this be accepted, at any rate provisionally, the problem which remains is to discover how this instinct has become so modified as to render possible the socialistic or even communistic behaviour of such societies as those of Melanesia.

The first question to be discussed is whether the instinct of acquisition, whose existence I assume, has been modified through the activity of some other instinct or by means of the influence of tradition and education.

* See *Instinct and the Unconscious*, 2nd edition, 1922, page 260.

If, in addition to the instinct prompting acquisition in the interest of the individual man also possesses an instinct prompting him to behaviour in the interest of the group, we should be provided with one possible mechanism by which the acquisitive instinct might be modified. Such an instinct, usually known as the herd-instinct, has in recent years been confidently assigned to man as part of his nature, but hitherto there have been singularly few attempts to justify the innate or instinctive character of the behaviour which has been ascribed to the activity of this instinct. We can be confident that this instinct exists in many species of animal, but we have no right to assume without inquiry that it exists in man. Elsewhere *
I have tried to show that spontaneity of social behaviour such as would be explicable through the activity of a herd-instinct is especially characteristic of such peoples as the Melanesian whom I have chosen to illustrate the existence of a socialistic society. But though Melanesian social behaviour suggests a relation between spontaneity of group-activity and socialistic practices, it does not of itself prove either the existence of an instinct or even of a special strength of such an instinct in the Melanesian. It is possible that the spontaneity of his group-activity

* The second lecture in this book.

is the result of the socialistic or group sentiments to which each member of such a society
is subjected from his earliest years. Moreover, if the existence of a herd-instinct in
man cannot be directly demonstrated in
a society where gregariousness is especially
strong, it is not likely to be demonstrated
from observation of the behaviour of such
an individualistic society as our own. The
existence of a herd-instinct in man, or perhaps
more correctly of an instinctive component
in the gregarious behaviour of man, will only
be demonstrated by the convergence and
agreement of lines of evidence from many
different fields of inquiry ; from the comparison of the behaviour of different societies ;
from observation of the behaviour of the
developing individual ; and from the study
of the disorders of the behaviour of the
individual when the subject of disease ; at
the same time we need a far more extensive
knowledge than we possess at present of
the relations between the behaviour of a
group as compared with the behaviour of
the individuals who make up the group.
Some light should be thrown upon the matter
by knowledge of the past history of the
social groupings of mankind. If the original
state of human society was of a kind now
exemplified by the Melanesian, it would
be far easier to understand man's possession
of a herd-instinct than if in the early stages

of human society he had the individualistic habits which seem to be characteristic of his nearest existing anthropoid relatives.

Here again I have no time to consider in any detail the evidence concerning the earliest form of grouping in human society but we can be fairly certain that before the development of agriculture and the domestication of animals man must have lived in small groups, probably corresponding closely in size and composition with the family, in which any close social cohesion could be explained through the activity of the parental instinct so that it would not be necessary to have recourse to any other form of herd-instinct for its explanation. There is much reason to believe that it was only when the development of agriculture made it possible for men to live together in much larger communities than were possible in the collecting stage that the clan-organisation with its many communistic features came into existence. One of the most difficult and disputable problems of anthropology is why the development of the clan-organisation should have been accompanied by its communistic features and by such high development of spontaneous group activity as we have some reason to associate with it. One possibility is that the development of the larger forms of social group again gave opportunity for the activity of an old herd-instinct which had lain dormant during the long period when the human group was little, if at all, larger than the family. It may also, of course, have been possible that the strong group-instinct or sentiment of the clan may have been only a development of that of the smaller family group, and that the differences in respect of the nature of ownership between such peoples as the Melanesians and ourselves depend on variations in the relative strengths of two conflicting sets of factors, those of an instinct of acquisition on one side and those, either instinctive or non-instinctive, which are associated with clan-organisation. Another quite different line of evidence concerning the existence or non-existence of a herd-instinct in man is derived from the phenomena of suggestion which is most readily explained as the manifestation of a gregarious instinct, but this also is a matter about which there is scope for difference of opinion. My own view developed in my book *Instinct and the Unconscious* is that the process of suggestion and its great influence on human behaviour, both in health and disease, provides one of the strongest lines of evidence in favour of the existence of a herd-instinct in man; but, as you probably all know, it has recently been held that the primary form of suggestion is an individual rather than a group pheno-menon, and this view has been accepted by many who still continue cheerfully to talk of the herd-instinct, apparently quite un-aware that in accepting the opinion of Baudouin they are largely, if not altogether, destroying the chief foundation upon which rests the existence of a herd-instinct in man.

Another most important line of evidence in favour of the existence of a herd-instinct in man is derived from the study of disease. In many forms of mental disorder there is great disturbance, or it may even be complete loss, of that regard for the opinion of the group which is now so often referred to the activity of a herd-instinct. Few of those who have dealt with pathological states from this point of view, however, show any signs of having tried to distinguish between instinctive and acquired aspects of behaviour or even to gain an elementary understanding of the nature of instinct. Thus, a recent writer of repute believes that in the consideration of instinct in relation to human behaviour it is a mistake to bring into the argument issues reached by the study of the behaviour of the lower animals, showing that he has wholly failed to understand the impossibility of any scientific treatment of instinct if the biological aspect of the subject is excluded.

Perhaps more important than the symptoms of definite disease are the quasi-pathological manifestations of the unorganised body of human beings, I do not call it a social group, which is now usually known as the crowd. Following Le Bon the interest of social psychologists has been largely directed to the impulsive, unregulated behaviour which is characteristic of a body of human beings who, under the stress of some disturbing conditions, act in common without the discipline which prepares the activity of the more organised forms of social grouping. The liability of the crowd to such undiscriminated and ungraduated modes of behaviour as panic, point definitely to such behaviour being the manifestation of deeply seated instinctive trends which are normally held in check by more recently acquired activities of the mind.

I must be content with this sketch of what I conceive to be the present position of the subject. In this brief paper I have first stated what I could, I believe, prove to your satisfaction if I had the time, that human societies vary greatly in respect of socialistic and individualistic social behaviour, and that some are just as closely wedded to socialistic practices as we are to individualism. I have, then, considered very briefly, indeed have done little more than enumerate, some of the lines of evidence to which we may look for the solution of the problems raised by these differences in the behaviour of human societies.

Even in stating these problems I have been

obliged to consider different possibilities which would arise after making certain assumptions. Thus, after accepting the position that there is an instinct of acquisition in the interest of the individual, I have stated different possibilities concerning the fate of this instinct among those peoples whose social system is definitely socialistic. As I have been driven to state the complicated problems which are involved, the whole matter bristles with assumptions, and throughout the treatment " possiblys " and " probablys " are scattered in profusion, while behind all one cannot help scenting the danger due to the preconceptions and prejudices inevitably aroused when such a subject as socialism is the topic of inquiry. We have here a subject the complexity of which is so great that it should certainly appeal to the members of a Critical Society, while it is also one which raises interesting questions of scientific method.

AN ADDRESS ON EDUCATION
AND MENTAL HYGIENE

V

I PROPOSE in what I say to you to-day to consider certain ways in which knowledge of the theory and art of medicine may be of service to the student of education. In recent years two great developments have taken place in medicine which bring it into much closer relations with education than was formerly the case. One of these is the greatly increased attention to hygiene, to prevention rather than cure, to use the words of the old adage; while the other great development, one especially active at the moment, is the application to disorders of the mind of principles similar to those which have long been applied to disorders of the body. I will begin by dealing briefly with these two developments. The state of disease is one which must have made a great impression on man from the time that he began to be aware that there lay in his hands some degree of control over his own destiny.

* An address prepared for delivery to students of education.

The early history of religion and magic probably turned largely upon man's attitude towards this striking vicissitude of his career and the still more catastrophic state of death to which it so often led. The magic and religion of existing backward races of mankind are full of features which show an intense interest in disease, but as a rule man was content to wait until disease presented itself in some guise or other before he took steps to avert the evil, and this pre-eminence of cure over prevention continued on into the Medicine of civilised peoples. It is only in our own days that we have come to put the prevention of disease in its proper place. There is little doubt that when the history of the Medicine of to-day comes to be written, its greatest achievement will not be found in the operative procedures, the antitoxins and the glandular extracts which bulk so largely in the estimation of the profession as well as of the laity, but in the systematic development of the public health service in our own country and the still more striking measures by which the tropical regions of the earth are being made available for the service of mankind in general.

The other great development, one of which I think we can be proud as the product of our generation, is the recognition that disorders of the mind are capable of being treated on lines very similar to those which we follow when dealing with the body. We are no longer content, as was the case until quite recently, to wait until the mind has fallen into total disorganisation, or has departed so widely from its healthy mode of working as to make seclusion necessary. We now recognise that mental disease, whether in its severer or slighter forms, is the outcome of processes following definite laws, and that by knowledge of these laws the sufferer may again be set upon the path of health.

It is a striking fact, and one which I intend to make the central point of what I have to say this afternoon, that one of the chief names which has been chosen for the curative process by which the sufferer is thus set upon this path of health is re-education. It is recognised that the process of psycho-therapy by which mental disorder is remedied is one in which the therapeutic process is of essentially the same kind as that by which the individual is normally adapted to social life.

It is a commonplace, expressed in the adage that outsiders see most of the game, that those who are immersed in any pursuit often fail to see tracks and openings which are at once apparent to one who comes from elsewhere and views the scene with unprejudiced eyes. I propose to-day to consider one or two lessons of psycho-therapy and of its process of re-education with the object of asking whether they may be of value to those who have not to wait until the mind has fallen into disorder, but whose function it is to put the individual from the beginning upon a track which will lead him into the path of health and keep him in that path.

The first lesson to be mentioned which has been learnt by the psychological medicine of to-day, perhaps the most important, concerns the vast importance of the influences which are brought to bear upon the individual in his earliest years. We are no longer content to adopt the pessimistic attitude of those who were fed on the old views of heredity, but we are coming to see to how great an extent the disorders and faulty trends of mental life are the result of wrong methods of treatment in the years when the individual is painfully learning to control the instinctive impulses which he has brought into the world with him so as to make them compatible with the traditions and ideals of the society of which he is to be a member. As I have said elsewhere, childhood is the prolonged scene of a conflict of this kind, and the outcome of the conflict depends largely on the process of education to which you are all about to devote your lives.

Though it is not difficult to see that while we can be confident that the process of education, taken in its broadest sense, largely determines the nature of the result of the conflict between instinctive trends and social ideals of which every human life is the scene, it is at present far more difficult to say with any confidence just how the knowledge derived from psychological medicine points the way to educational method. One or two lines, however, are fairly clear, and I propose to-day to consider briefly one lesson which can, I think, be utilised.

In order to make this line clear I must go back a little and consider two broad lines upon principles underlying the methods of psycho-therapy. In the early stages of psychological medicine the chief stress was laid on suggestion, of which hypnotism was the most striking form. Faith and suggestion are still the prominent agencies in most lines of psycho-therapeutical treatment. It is altogether to them that are due any beneficial results which may have come from the sensational methods of Coué, of which so much has been recently heard, and those processes form the basis of much of the treatment methods practised to-day. It is now one feature of these two processes and of methods founded upon them that they make no attempt to reach the root of the disorder, in the treatment of which they are applied ; but their advocates are content to treat the outward and obvious manifestations usually called symptoms.

When M. Coué tells his devotees to say that

their pains are growing less and their appetite greater every day, he makes no attempt to discover the causal factors upon which the pains or the diminished appetite depend. Using the language of ordinary medicine, the treatment is purely palliative. The main principle of modern medicine, that if symptoms only are treated while the cause of the symptoms is left untouched, the trouble will probably recur sooner or later, perhaps even in far more troublesome guise than that for which the palliative remedies were originally applied. The second main line of treatment is that which recognises this principle and makes it its chief business to discover the nature of disorder, one often dating back for many years, through whose activity the symptoms are produced. Its object is that the sufferer shall come to understand the faulty trends by which his disorder has been produced and by such self-knowledge shall see where his life has left the normal path and how his steps can again be set upon the path of health. It is this process which is denoted when the physician speaks of the process of re-education.

I wish to-day to draw your attention to a difference of the most important kind between these two lines of treatment of disorders of the mind. In the second case the patient is led to know himself, to understand the nature of the process by which his life has been disturbed, and to see for himself how he can overcome the difficulties which have led him away from health and sanity. By this process he learns self, not only to understand and foresee conditions which may again lead him astray, but, even more important, he learns to be self-reliant and confident in his own strength and knowledge, and not to lean on others. In the methods which rely on faith and suggestion, on the other hand, there is inevitably produced a state of dependence, sometimes dependence on another personality, sometimes dependence on some line of action which is believed to have an intrinsic value of precisely the same order as that which gives to the savage his faith in the magic that so often dominates his life.

Now, I expect by this time you will all see where I have been leading. We all know two kinds of teaching and two kinds of teacher. There is the teacher who lays down the law in an emphatic tone and expects to be believed with such assurance that his expectations are largely realised. He succeeds in making his pupils replicas, perhaps even successful replicas of himself ; and since a teacher of this class is usually one who would be hard put to defend his views if they were criticised, he thus tends to perpetuate not only false attitude towards life but also second-rate or outworn opinions.

The other kind of teacher is he who, when putting a case, gives the evidence on either side as impartially as he can and leads his pupils to see how opinions are formed. He gives them strength and knowledge to deal with the many difficult situations by which they must sooner or later be confronted. Not only does such a teacher produce the qualities of true knowledge and self-reliance, but he puts his pupils into a position to understand, if not to originate, solutions of the problems which are continually arising in such a progressive society as our own.

I believe that the two cases of the psychotherapeutist and the teacher which I have cited are not only closely if not exactly parallel in their methods, but there is the further likeness that in their respective walks of life one path is far easier than the other and also more attractive. To most people, whether they be physicians or teachers, it is far more attractive to be looked up to as a fountain of wisdom and to be regarded as an oracle than to run the danger of having one's views or line of treatment discredited by a critical or pupil patient. As a matter of fact one meets with a hundred teachers of the dogmatic and dependent kind for one who acts in what I believe to be the higher and more promising way. I shall give you two examples to illustrate the kind of thing I mean. Not long ago at a meeting of the Psychological Society my friend Dr Myers read a paper one part of which I criticised. There was present a well-known medical teacher so distinguished that he had been knighted, who got up and said that he had come to the meeting expecting to be instructed by two such eminent authorities as Myers and myself, and that he had been horrified at finding that instead of being told by us what was the truth he had found us disagreeing with one another.

The other example is that of a well-known university teacher who, in my presence, was heard objecting to Wells's *Outlines of History*, because he gave footnotes which disagreed with the text. How disturbing, he said, it must be to the students' mind !

Now it is evident that neither of these two distinguished men, each of whom had given his life to teaching, had even a glimmer of understanding of the fact that the aim of education is not to inspire blind confidence and faith, but to fit men and women to deal with the situations of life, and especially with those situations with which they are confronted as members of a society so complicated and so full of difficult problems as our own. It is the attitude of such men that is directly responsible for the credulity with which the nation swallows the arguments and nostrums of a Yellow Press, allows itself to be swindled by the unscrupulous company promoters, and remains incompetent to engage in logical argument or consistent thought.

AN ADDRESS ON "THE AIMS OF ETHNOLOGY"

VI

I WANT this evening to tell you what the science of ethnology is trying to do, and how it hopes to contribute to the general sum of knowledge. I shall also speak of some of its needs if it is to fulfil these aims.

It is the business of ethnology to study the nature of the different groups, whether we call them nations, tribes, or what not, into which Man has come to be divided. Each of these groups, even the simplest tribe of Australia or Tierra del Fuego, has a complex character and shows features of culture, such as language, social organisation, religion, arts and crafts, each of which forms a special subject of study. Some of these studies, such as philology and sociology, are already advanced enough to have received names, and form mental disciplines recognised in the universities and schools. It is the task

* This lecture was originally prepared for the instruction of students of anthropology in Cambridge, but during the last three years Dr Rivers had delivered it in many universities and schools in England and America.

of ethnology to study these subjects, not as abstract isolated branches of human culture, but to consider them comprehensively as manifestations of the activities of groups of mankind. Its special aim is to understand the relation of these groups to one another, not only at the present time, but in the past. It is its business to discover how it has come about that man presents his vast diversity of speech and thought and custom, and to find the explanation of the many points of similarity which constantly present themselves throughout the diversity. I can perhaps best illustrate the nature and aims of the science by a brief record of its history, a history even now of very short duration.

So long as it was universally believed that man came into existence by a special act of creation, and owed his diversity of speech and custom to the miracle of Babel, there was little scope for a science of ethnology. It was generally held in the past that the more backward peoples of the earth, or rather those whom we regard as backward because they are different from ourselves, were so because they had degenerated from the state in which they were created. Moreover, when people speculated concerning the similarities and diversities of human culture, it is easy to understand why they should ascribe the similarities to such dispersals as tend to follow the great catastrophes of human history. It was even natural that such similarities as were especially familiar through the Biblical record should be ascribed to the dispersal of the Jews. The frequent belief in the widespread influence of the lost Ten Tribes was, in the then state of the subject, a legitimate view for which it was even possible to provide some evidence.

When the subject began to be studied about fifty years ago by those trained in scientific methods, this line of thought was dominant, and the work of the writers of that time, such as Meadows Taylor,* Lane-Fox,† Fergusson,‡ Park Harrison,§ and Miss Buckland,¶ was guided by the idea that civilised man had travelled far over the world and that the similarities found in widely-separated parts of the earth are the outcome of the diffusion of features of culture from some part of the world, the special conditions of which had led to their appearance and development.

* Meadows Taylor, " On Prehistoric Archæology of India," *Journ. Ethnol. Soc.*, New Series, vol. i., 1868-9.
† A. Lane-Fox, " Remarks on Mr Hodder Westropp's Paper on Cromlechs, with a Map of the World, showing the Distribution of Megalithic Monuments."
‡ *Rude Stone Monuments*, London, 1872.
§ " On the Artificial Enlargement of the Earlobe," *Journ. Anthropol. Inst.*, vol. ii., 1872-3, page 190.
¶ A. W. Buckland, " The Serpent in Connection with Primitive Metallurgy," *Journ. Anthropol. Inst.*, vol. iv., 1874-5. *Ibid.*, " Ethnological Hints afforded by the Stimulants in use among Savages and among the Ancients," *Journ. Anthropol. Inst.*, vol. viii., 1878-9. *Ibid.*, " On Tattooing," *Journ. Anthropol. Inst.*, vol. xvii., 1887-8.

About forty years ago a great change took place in the opinions of those who devoted themselves to the study of human culture and society. The idea of evolution, which was then slowly forging its way into general acceptance, became an article of almost universal belief among students of anthropology ; and as the result of a misunderstanding of what exactly biologists meant by evolution, they put forward the remarkable claim that, after an original dispersal, which they did not attempt to explain, the different varieties of mankind had developed their cultures independently. They accepted the doctrine of the German traveller and ethnologist, Adolf Bastian, that the similarities between the beliefs and customs of different peoples are due to the uniformity of the constitution of the human mind, so that, given similar conditions of climate and conditions of life, the same modes of thought and behaviour come into existence independently, which are in no way due to the influence of one people upon another. When I began the study of ethnology twenty years ago this point of view had become absolutely dominant, at any rate in this country and America, and I accepted it without question. In common with others, I believed in the doctrine that similarities of thought and custom throughout the world arose through similarity of external conditions, and ignored the obvious fact that the similarities are found amidst external conditions of the most diverse kind —in islands and continents ; in tropical and in temperate climates ; among agricultural, hunting, and pastoral peoples ; while, on the other hand, diversities are found within regions uniform in climate and social habit, while in many parts of the earth diversities of the most striking kind are found within a region only a few square miles in size.

It may be instructive to consider for a moment one or two considerations which greatly contributed to strengthen the belief in independent origin. One was the absence or very imperfect character of the means of navigation in parts of the world where, if there had been external influence at all this must have come by sea. Thus, the idea that no influence can have reached America across the Pacific Ocean seemed to receive support from the absence of any but the rudest forms of sea-craft along the whole of the western shore of the continent. This was put forward as a cogent piece of evidence that the great Inca culture of Peru, with its very advanced character, and in spite of its many points of close resemblance with cultures of the Old World, was nevertheless the independent outcome of the fertility and ingenuity of mind of the indigenous inhabitants of America. It was only necessary to show, as I was able to do,* that there are well-established cases, even among the inhabitants of islands, where the art of navigation has once existed and has disappeared. If the inhabitants of islands can give up an industry which would seem to be essential to their welfare, there is no great difficulty in assuming the degeneration or even disappearance of the art of navigation among the inhabitants of the coasts of a continent.

This special case is only one example of the neglect of the factor of degeneration in human culture. So long as students were under the influence of the idea of special creation, degeneration was the chief agency by which features of human culture were explained, but with the incoming of the idea of evolution this factor was thrown wholly on one side, or was used only to explain relatively unimportant facts. There was a complete failure to appreciate the vast part which degeneration is continually playing in the history of human institutions.

It may be noted at this point that, though Germany must be regarded as the home of the idea of independent origin, there has never been the unanimity of acceptance of the doctrine in that country which was at one time present here and in America. Ratzel, the author of a large popular work on the

* "The Disappearance of Useful Arts," *Festskrift t. Edvard Westermarck*, Helsingfors, 1912, page 109.

Early History of Mankind, was an advocate
of the view that similarities of culture are
due to transmission from some centre of
origin, and during the early years of the present century a school grew up in Germany, of
which Graebner * and Ankermann † were the
most important members, which attempted
to formulate a definite scheme of a succession
of cultures which had spread over the world
and produced the wide distribution of many
elements of culture. This work was almost
completely disregarded in this country, and
the movement which has taken place here in
favour of transmission as the source of
similarities of human culture has been independently worked out during the last ten
years on lines wholly different from those of
the German ethnologists.

In describing this movement it will be best
to begin with the work of Elliot Smith.
In the course of anatomical investigation
of a large number of mummies from many
different periods of Egyptian history, it
became evident that at the beginning of the
third millennium B.C. there had been an
invasion of people from the north with heads
somewhat rounder than those of the pre-

* " Kulturkreise u. Kulturschichten in Ozeanien," *Zeitschr. f.
Ethnol.*, xxxvii., 1905, page 39 ; " Die melanesische Bogen-
kultur u. ihre Verwandten," *Anthropos*, iv., 1909, page 726 and
O. 998.
† " Kulturkreise u. Kulturschichten in Afrika," *Zeitschr. f.
Ethnol.*, xxxvii., 1905, page 54.

dynastic inhabitants of the country, and with features of the skull of the kind now usually known as Armenoid.* When Elliot Smith returned to England he found that skulls of the same type as those which had made their way into Egypt from the north were numerous in Europe, including these islands, but at first no evidence presented itself to his notice in favour of a wider distribution. On coming to Cambridge to examine, however, in 1911, Elliot Smith found skulls with definite Armenoid characters among those put out to test the candidates. These skulls had once belonged to natives of the Chatham Islands, south of New Zealand, a place almost as remote from Egypt or Armenia as could well be found. Being thus led to entertain the idea of extensive movements of early man about the earth, Elliot Smith studied the distribution of certain features of culture, such as mummification and megalithic architecture, in which he had become interested during his stay in Egypt. He found features of distribution which led him to believe that these two manifestations of human activity had arisen in Egypt and spread therefrom to the many parts of the earth where they are now found.† The distribution of megalithic monuments especi-

---

* *The Ancient Egyptians and Their Influence upon the Civilisation of Europe*, London, 1911, page 95.
† *The Migrations of Early Culture*, Manchester, 1915.

ally pointed to their builders having travelled in the main by sea,* so that the nature of the means of navigation became of great importance. It was at this stage that I was able to contribute by showing, as I have already mentioned, that even so essential an art as navigation is not immune from the process of degeneration.

About the time that Elliot Smith was engaged in working out the evidence for the world-wide spread of mummification and megalithic architecture, I was studying material brought back from an expedition to Melanesia in 1908.† This study led me to the view that Melanesian culture could only be explained on the supposition that there had been a succession of intruding peoples, one of which had brought with it the practice of preserving the dead and the making of megalithic monuments. I made it my business to try to ascertain the kind of process which takes place when such elements of culture from outside, perhaps of a relatively advanced order, are introduced among so rude a people as the Melanesians. I came to the conclusion that most of the social practices of Melanesia are the result of the interaction between the beliefs and customs of immi-

* See W. H. R. Rivers, " The Contact of Peoples," *Essays and Studies presented to William Ridgeway*, Cambridge, 1913, page 489.
† *Rep. Brit. Assoc.*, Portsmouth, 1911, page 490 ; *The History of Melanesian Society*, Cambridge, 1914.

grant and indigenous peoples ; that when a strange custom brought by an immigrant people so takes the fancy of the indigenous population that they adopt it as their own, it suffers great modification, sometimes in the direction of development, and sometimes of such a kind that we can only regard the result as degeneration. I was led to the view that the current concept of independent evolution, which I had accepted so blindly, was a fiction. The evidence from Melanesia points to advance as taking place only under external influence, and to a mode of development in which isolation spells stagnation. It suggests that an isolated people do not invent or advance, but that the introduction of new ideas, new instruments, and new techniques leads to a definite process of evolution, the products of which may differ greatly from either the indigenous or the immigrant constituents, the result of the interaction thus resembling a chemical compound rather than a physical mixture. The study of Melanesian culture suggests that when this newly set up process of evolution has reached a certain pitch it comes to an end, and is followed by a period of stagnation which endures until some fresh incoming of external influence starts anew a period of progress.

In working out our schemes of transmission and evolution, Elliot Smith and I were met by two serious difficult.es, one of a more special, the other of a more general kind. Both of these difficulties have been surmounted through the work of W. J. Perry. The more special difficulty is concerned with the distribution of megalithic monuments, which forms so excellent a touchstone of the rival views. Elliot Smith and I found definite reason to believe that the megalithic art, together with a cult of the sun, had found their way from Europe or Asia into Oceania,* and passing still farther across the Pacific had influenced the culture of America, and especially of Peru. In going from India to Oceania the mariners who carried the art of building these rude stone monuments must have passed through the East Indian, or, as it is often called, the Malay Archipelago. If our views are to hold good, there should be evidence of their handiwork in the islands of this region. Such evidence was generally believed to be absent, and this supposed absence had so impressed one advocate of the unity of the megalithic culture, Professor J. Macmillan Brown, of New Zealand,† that he advanced the view that the culture had spread across the continent of Asia, and had then reached the islands of the Pacific by way of Japan. Mr Perry undertook a com-

* G. Elliot Smith, *op. cit.* ; W. H. R. Rivers, " Sun-cult and Megaliths in Oceania," *American Anthropologist* (N.S.), vol. xvii., 1915, page 431.
† *Maori and Polynesian*, London, 1907.

plete survey of the Indonesian evidence.* He found, in the first place, that in certain islands of the East Indian Archipelago, especially in Sumba, there were monuments, in the form of dolmens, closely resembling those of other parts of the world, but that these had a more limited distribution than we should expect if this archipelago had been the pathway of the carriers of the megalithic culture. He therefore turned his attention to the distribution of stone-work in general in Indonesia, and found a remarkable correspondence between it and certain other elements of culture, the general distribution of which had led Elliot Smith to connect them with the megalithic art. Perry came to the conclusion that megalithic monuments were few in Indonesia, because the culture of their makers had suffered great modification in this region, so that the art of stone-working, which elsewhere had expended itself in monuments of vast size, had been here content to make stone seats and stone offering places, and to use stone in the construction of graves. It is possible that a larger number of definitely megalithic remains may yet be found in Indonesia, but in the meantime Perry has shown reason to believe that their scarcity is due to some conditions which led people, attaching great importance to the use of stone in their religious rites, to practise

* *The Megalithic Culture of Indonesia*, Manchester, 1918.

their art in a more modest fashion than in their original home, and even more modest than in regions farther to the east.

The other contribution made by Perry is of still greater importance. When the facts began to lead us to the view that in remote ages man had undertaken voyages to the most distant parts of the earth, it was difficult to see what could have acted as his motive. About this time geologists and archæologists had put forward the view that there had been a periodical drying up of Asia, and Huntington especially had written about it under the metaphorical title, *The Pulse of Asia*.* Such a drying up would have led to a great displacement of population, a displacement to which silent witness is borne by the large and once populous cities now buried in the sands of the central Asiatic desert.

Believers in the wide movements of man throughout the world were inclined to ascribe his early migrations to the need for home and food, brought into existence by the desolation of a region which must have housed and fed vast numbers of people. Such a need might account for pressure of population in other parts of Asia, or even for movements such as we know to have taken place eastwards to the Malay Archipelago, and westwards into Africa. It is difficult

* London, 1907.

121

to see, however, how any pressure of population in Asia can have produced movements which led men as far afield as the islands of the Pacific and the continent of America.

However remote the age with which we are dealing, it is always useful to look at home for the clue to motives which have guided the behaviour of man. If we had done this, we should not have been so long in discovering the motives of the megalithic wandering. It was reserved for Perry to find this motive. Elliot Smith had, at the beginning of 1915, mapped out the areas which he knew, or inferred, to have been the seats of megalithic influence. He sent Perry a copy of this map. About the same time he informed him that Mrs Zelia Nuttall had claimed that the founders of American civilisation had shown a special appreciation of pearls and precious metals. A chance examination of an economic atlas enabled Perry to combine these two items of information, for he saw that the distribution of pearl-shell in the Pacific Ocean agreed so nearly with Elliot Smith's megalithic areas that the presence of pearls would provide a sufficient motive for the settlements in these regions. Further examination showed that, in inland areas, the chief motive for the megalithic settlements was supplied by the presence of gold and other forms of wealth. He therefore put forward the view that the motive which had led the ancient voyagers so far afield was precisely that which acts as the essential stimulus to our own migrations, viz., the search for objects needed to satisfy human needs, material, æsthetic and religious.* In our own case it is chiefly the satisfaction of material needs which has led us to the far-distant regions of the earth, though the extent of the missionary movement and the great part taken by this movement in the spread of our culture show that material needs have not stood alone. In the earlier movements of mankind it is probable that needs of a religious kind, or, at any rate, of a less material kind, were more prominent, and that even such an object as gold was sought because of its supposed magical or religious properties long before it became the vehicle of currency. It is probable that one of the earliest motives which led men widely about the world was the search for an elixir of life by which to restore youth and prolong human existence.†

As might be expected, it has been found that the correspondence between the distribution of gold workings and megalithic monuments is not exact, but where such stone structures occur dissociated from gold there are usually other objects of wealth which would have acted as the motives for settle-

---

* "The Relationship between the Geographical Distribution of Megalithic Monuments and Ancient Mines," *Mem. and Proc. Manchester Lit. and Phil. Soc.*, 1915.

† G. Elliot Smith, *The Evolution of the Dragon*, Manchester, 1919.

ment. Thus, round the shores of the Baltic, where megalithic monuments abound but gold is absent, there is the amber, which, through its supposed religious or magical properties, had so great an attraction for man in early times that the ancient trade in amber between the north and south of Europe continued far into the Middle Ages.

In other parts of the world, such as the shores of Southern India and in some parts of the Pacific, it would seem, as has been said, that pearls and pearl-shell were the attraction, while there is reason to believe that elsewhere spices and odorous resins, needed to embalm the dead, were among the objects sought by these ancient explorers of the seven seas. Mr Perry is now engaged in the more minute comparison of the distribution of gold working with that of megalithic monuments and of other elements of culture, such as terraced irrigation, which are associated with them.

He will be much encouraged in his quest by recent * work in a field which would seem at first sight a most unlikely region to furnish confirmation of his hypothesis. In New Guinea, perhaps the least known and wildest of all the larger regions of the world, various objects in stone have been found,†

* This lecture was written in 1919.
† C. G. Seligmann and T. A. Joyce, " On Primitive Objects in British New Guinea," *Anthropological Essays presented to Edward Burnett Tylor*, Oxford, 1907, page 325.

often buried away feet below the surface of the ground, mortars and pestles being especially prominent among the objects so found. The present natives disclaim all knowledge of the art by which such objects were made, and ascribe their manufacture to a people who long ago came and settled among them. Lieut. Chinnery, to whom we owe much of our knowledge of these objects and of the beliefs of the natives about them,[*] has pointed out that these examples of native stone-work have been found chiefly on gold-bearing districts, and that in some cases there are stone-circles or other forms of ancient stone-work in the neighbourhood. Mr Chinnery has suggested that the pestles and mortars were used by their makers to crush the quartz from which they extracted the precious substance in the quest of which they had ventured so far afield.

Now that accumulating evidence is pointing so clearly to early voyages comparable, both in motive and extent, with those of our own epoch, we are naturally beginning to speculate about the original home of the culture which was thus diffused, about the race of the voyagers, and about the date at which the voyages occurred. Of these three problems, that which is most open to investigation, and is at the same time essential

[*] " Stone-work and Goldfields in British New Guinea," *Journ. Roy. Anthropol. Inst.*, vol. xlix., 1919, page 271.

to the solution of the other two, is the centre from which such practices as megalithic architecture, sun-cult, mummification of the dead, and irrigation were diffused.

From the beginning of his work Elliot Smith has insisted, in the face of bitter opposition and even obloquy, that this original home was Egypt. He believed that the geographical features of this country furnish just such conditions as were needed to bring into existence the practices which have been so widely diffused. Thus, to take mummification as an example, we know that the special character of the soil of Egypt preserved so completely for thousands of years the bodies of the dead pre-dynastic Egyptians who were interred in the contracted position, that Elliot Smith has been able to study the structure even of so perishable an organ as the brain.* When the idea arose of placing the bodies of the dead in rock-cut tombs, or in structures representing the house, there would no longer be the close contact of the body with the soil which was essential to this preservation, and some kind of artificial process became necessary to prevent the

* *Journ. of Anat. and Physiol.*, vol. xxxvi., 1902, page 375.
[It was Dr Rivers himself who, in 1900, first called my attention to the preservation of the brain in pre-dynastic Egyptian bodies, and thus incidentally introduced me to anthropological investigation. At the time he was working at the problems of colour vision of the natives in Upper Egypt, and happened to see desiccated brains in the skulls brought to light there by Dr Randall-MacIver.—G. E. S.]

natural decay. Thus was started a process by the development of which arose the practice of mummification of the dead, the full history of which in Egypt has been worked out by Elliot Smith.* During a visit to Australia just before the outbreak of the war, he had an opportunity of examining a mummy from the islands of Torres Straits, between Australia and New Guinea, and found that when preserving their dead the inhabitants of these islands made incisions in the flank or perineum, and sutured the wounds so made in just the same places and manner as were customary at a certain period of Egyptian history. Moreover, they extracted the brain substance through the foramen magnum, and made incisions on the extremities just as was done in Egypt at this period.†

This correspondence in the details of an art is of great importance as evidence of transmission, for it is difficult to explain it on any hypothesis other than that the art spread from one place to the other. The old view that these details were discovered independently in Torres Straits would make it necessary to believe that, in a climate where decomposition of the dead sets in a few hours after death, the rude savages of Torres Straits discovered a technique which cost the

* See references in *The Migrations of Early Culture*, pages 141-2.
† *The Migrations of Early Culture*, page 21.

highly cultured Egyptian of dynastic times many centuries of patient trial and research.

Elliot Smith had already shown * that the dolmens found in different parts of Europe have details of structure which point to their derivation from the mastaba, the original flat-topped superstructure of the Egyptian tomb of the Pyramid age. At one end of many dolmens there is a stone with a hole in it, and Elliot Smith believes that this represents the opening in the front of the mastaba through which food was passed to feed the dead lying within, while a structure which may be called the antechapel of the mastaba is often, though vaguely, represented in dolmens in front of the holed stone. Again, in Egypt the sun has an important place in the culture of the kings who made the great Pyramids of Egypt, and it is not necessary to insist on reasons why Egypt was the birthplace of irrigation. Geographical and climatic conditions made the association of these four practices natural in Egypt. If the culture of which they form part was carried about the world it will explain the presence of this association in regions where it is impossible to find any adequate motive for their origin by a process of independent evolution.

As I have already said, the view of Elliot

* " The Evolution of the Rock-cut Tomb and the Dolmen," *Essays and Studies presented to William Ridgeway*, Cambridge, 1913, page 493.

Smith that Egypt was the original home of the megalithic culture has met with the most bitter opposition, but every year is tending to confirm its truth. The Rev. C. E. Fox, a missionary in the Solomon Islands, has, during the last few months,* sent us an account of the burial customs of the people of San Cristoval and other neighbouring islands in that region. He tells us that the dead of the chiefly clan, called the Araha, were buried on the top of mounds, made sometimes of stone, sometimes of earth. These mounds often tend to be pyramidal in shape, and in this case resemble almost exactly the flat-topped mastaba of Egypt. The body of the dead chief is placed in a recess within the mound, and a shaft leads from the surface of the mound to this recess, exactly as in the mastaba and pyramids of Egypt. On the top of the mound of San Cristoval there is often a structure composed of a table stone resting on three or four uprights, having thus the characteristic form of a dolmen. Under or by this dolmen is an image in human form, carved out of coral or stone, which is believed to represent the dead man and to act as the abiding-place of the ghost which left his body at his death. Not only does this image reproduce exactly one of the most characteristic features of the mortuary customs of the ancient Egyptian, but Mr

* This refers to 1919.

129

Fox draws our attention to a special feature of the statues of San Cristoval which presents a most striking resemblance in point of detail with those of Egypt. The statues are seated, and at the back of the head there is a structure like a pig-tail which reaches down to the stone surface upon which the statue is placed. Mr Fox writes to ask what this strange feature, quite unlike any existing head-dress of Melanesia, can mean, unaware that he is describing an almost exact representation of a similar feature of the statues of Cheops, Chephren, and Mycerinus, the builders of the great Pyramids of Egypt.

One more detail. On the back of the Egyptian statues there is usually the representation of a falcon (often called an eagle or hawk). In San Cristoval the chiefs of the Araha whose bodies are buried in the flat-topped mounds have the eagle as their totem.

Moreover, the preservation of the bodies which are buried in these tombs is assisted by removing the abdominal viscera through an incision in the flank, exactly as was done in ancient Egypt. The resemblance between the mortuary customs of ancient Egypt and modern San Cristoval, so close and extending to so many points of detail, makes it incredible that they should have arisen independently in these two regions. We can be confident that mariners imbued with the culture of Egypt, if they were not themselves Egyptians, reached the Solomon Islands in their search for wealth, and that their funeral rites so impressed the people of these far-distant isles that they have persisted to this day.

It is a striking fact that the Solomon Islands were so named by the Spanish explorers of the sixteenth century who, having subdued the people of Central America, set out on further voyages of exploration across the Pacific, in order to discover the countries from which King Solomon obtained the gold and precious stones and timbers for the building of the temple. Finding these islands after their long voyage across the Pacific, they named them after the monarch whose enterprise they were seeking to emulate. After this brief visit of the Spaniards, the islands again passed out of our ken until the last century, and now we learn that the Spanish voyagers were somewhere near the truth when they named the islands after the Hebrew king, and that this region had indeed been reached, not by King Solomon's mariners, but by voyagers from one or other of the early civilisations of the Orient. Which of these civilisations furnished the home of these early wanderers it is not at present possible to say, but it may be of interest to dwell for a moment on the problem of the date at which the wanderings occurred. I must in the first place note that Egyptian history provides us with our instruments for the dating of all the early civilisations of the world. If the culture of so remote and savage a region as the Solomon Islands has been influenced by Egypt, it may be possible by the nature of this influence to tell at the least when the early travellers set out upon the journey by which they were to plant their culture in such distant countries. Just as we now date a stratum of the remains of Cnossos by a sherd of Egyptian pottery, or a building of Palestine or Elam by the discovery of an Egyptian scarab, so may we hope to give an approximate date to customs or institutions of Melanesia or aboriginal America by the discovery of such practices as those which Mr Fox is now recording.

I have now sketched only too briefly the process by which ethnology has attained its present state. I should like next to consider —it must be very briefly—where we hope that the science may come to stand in the general scheme of learning. In the first place, we believe that if we succeed in discovering the historical processes by which human activity has produced the existing cultures of the earth, we shall then be provided with a mass of material by the study of which we can formulate the laws which direct and govern the activities and fate of those groups, whether we call them tribes, nations, or empires, into which the peoples of the earth are divided, as well as the laws which determine the growth of the social customs and institutions of mankind.

The science of ethnology may well put before it another goal. The records of our own past, and of the past of the great peoples from whom so much of our own culture is derived, are very incomplete, especially on the psychological side. We have no direct means of learning how these ancient peoples felt and thought, except through literary records. Excavations will doubtless yet bring to light many new documents, while the decipherment of the scripts and hieroglyphs of the Cretans, Hittites, and other long-perished peoples will doubtless some day add greatly to our knowledge. But there will always be large gaps in this knowledge, due to the imperfection of the literary record. Is it too bold a wish that some of these gaps may be supplied by our knowledge of the ideas, sentiments, and beliefs of the far-distant savages who still preserve habits and customs brought to them in long-past ages? Is it too much to hope that peoples who have preserved with such fidelity the material customs of those who once settled among them may have preserved with at least equal fidelity the social and religious beliefs of their visitors? If these hopes should be realised, the study of even the rudest people of to-day may contribute to our understanding of those ancient cultures of Egypt,

Sumer, Elam, and Babylon, which, through their influence upon the Jews, have had so great an effect, not only on our religion, but on our ethical and social traditions. The people of Indonesia, New Guinea, and Melanesia hold beliefs concerning the duality of the soul which closely resemble those lately revealed by the study of the Pyramid texts as having been held in Egypt, and the study of rude beliefs concerning death, the life after death, and other mysteries may well supply links by which we may fill gaps in the literary record.

Before I finish I must say a word about the present situation of the science of ethnology in relation to its needs. This science has in one respect a unique position, and one which should arouse the interest, if not the compassion, of anyone who cares for learning. We have only begun to understand how to collect the rich store of material presented by the cultures of the outlying places of the earth at a moment when these cultures are rapidly vanishing. The movement of our civilisation which has put this rich store of material within our sight, if not yet within our grasp, has at the same time carried with it the seeds of a deadly disease by which this material is being swept away. The Tasmanians, a people closely allied to, but yet differing in many respects from, the Australian aborigines, are already gone. The Bushmen, the last representatives of a people once widely spread over Africa, and probably, as palæolithic art suggests, over parts of Europe, too, are almost gone, and only survive here and there in small numbers in inhospitable regions, such as the Kalahari Desert, where their complete extinction cannot be long delayed. The Hottentot, of equal interest in the past history of Africa, and possibly of much significance in the history of Egypt, will soon follow the Bushman. In the region I know best, in Melanesia and Polynesia, many tribes have already disappeared.* On my last visit to the New Hebrides I heard of just three natives left in the island of Aore, on whose coast sherds of pottery bear witness that not long ago it bore a numerous and thriving population. In the island of Espiritu Santo I visited the Vulua tribe, which twenty years ago, according to the estimate of Mr Bowie, the intrepid and learned missionary of that district, numbered two hundred people. I found a wretched remnant of fifteen to twenty people so degraded and hopeless that I failed to arouse any interest in their customs, and had to be content with a few specimens of their language. This differed so greatly from that of surrounding tribes as to show that if they had been visited ten years ago we should have

* On this subject see *Essays on the Depopulation of Melanesia* edited by W. H. R. Rivers, Cambridge, 1922.

obtained a record of a culture which might have supplied links to assist us to understand the past history of the island. Ten years hence there will almost certainly be dozens of tribes in the same state as those of Aore or Vulua. Even if, more fortunate, they manage to maintain life and material prosperity, their beliefs and the knowledge of their ancient culture will certainly disappear, for it is only from the old men of such peoples that information of value can be obtained. With every old man who dies in Melanesia there goes, and goes for ever, knowledge which the scholars of the future will regard as of inestimable worth. The two men who helped me most during my visit to Melanesia twelve years ago were already dead before I had been able to publish the facts which through their devoted interest I was able to record. Lately I have heard that the man from whom I learnt most in my visit to the New Hebrides only seven years ago is already dead, a victim to dysentery, which forms perhaps the most potent instrument for the undoing of the people. I have told you this evening of work which shows how rich a treasure-house of knowledge exists in Melanesia, knowledge now easily accessible and only waiting to be garnered. Often it exists in a form which suggests the nuggets of a gold-field, but differing from the metal in being so evanescent that it will disappear for ever if not transmuted into the lasting monument provided by the written word. Perhaps some of you as administrators, missionaries, or doctors will go to places where these treasures are waiting for collection, and in such case you will, I hope, be able to spare time and trouble to learn how to collect and record the facts of which the science of ethnology has so great a need. Perhaps there are here some to whom the lure of the past makes such appeal that they may give themselves wholly to the task of adding to the small but growing pile of knowledge by which the early history of mankind may be revealed.

A NOTE ON "THE AIMS OF ETHNOLOGY"

By G. ELLIOT SMITH, F.R.S.

ETHNOLOGY AND PSYCHOLOGY

A NOTE ON "THE AIMS OF ETHNOLOGY"

HOWEVER the disciplines of the study of man and the study of the human mind may seem to differ the one from the other, it has always been recognised that the investigation of custom and belief cannot be wholly divorced from psychology : but during the last decade Freud and his followers have become involved in an intrigue with ethnology which threatens disaster to both parties, and under no circumstances can lead to a stable union. The new teaching in ethnology, which is explained in the article by the late Dr Rivers in this number, destroys the foundation of the belief in the reality of "typical symbols," and brings to the ground the fantastic speculations built upon it by Freud and Jung.

The history of Freud's teaching is rich in contradictions and illogical claims. But the most remarkable feature of this great reform in psychological method is the fact that most of the opposition aroused against it has been the result of Freud's departure from his own principles. The essence of his innovation was the fact that he took quite seriously the patient's symptoms, his phantasies and his dreams, and made a real attempt to discover how they originated and to explain their significance. But after pursuing this aim up to a certain point and illuminating the patient's beliefs in the light of his individual experience, the Freudian psychologist suddenly, and quite inconsequently, throws overboard all the essential principles of Freud's great reform, and attempts to force these products of the individual mind into conformity with something that is not the result of experience. He assumes certain instinctive modes of reaction and certain hereditarily transmitted impulses towards symbolisation, which are foreign alike to any serious psychologist's conception of instinct, or to the knowledge of any man in the street as to the origin of symbols. To bolster up claims that are in themselves utterly preposterous, as well as contrary to the essence of his own teaching—*i.e.* of the dominating influence of individual experience—Freud called in the aid of the orthodox doctrines of ethnology, unfortunately for him, at the moment when, as Dr Rivers explains in his article, they were beginning to crumble.

During the last half-century ethnologists have become more and more committed to the view that the similarities in custom and belief so strikingly displayed in the early civilisations of widely-scattered peoples might have been brought about, not by the diffusion of knowledge and example from one group of people to another, but by the independent development of these likenesses as the result of some innate quality of the human mind. There is nothing new in this doctrine. It was being taught in 1788 by Dr William Robertson, Principal of the University of Edinburgh,* and again in 1835 by Hugh Miller : but it was not until Bastian (1860) decked it out in the terminology of misapplied Herbartian philosophy that any attention was given to this remarkable fallacy. Bastian's *Völker-Gedanken* can truly be regarded as the parents of the " typical symbols " of the Freudian doctrine. Bastian's theories, put forward in uncouth and unusually obscure German, attracted little notice until Tylor adopted them and gave them expression in lucid English. This did not happen until Tylor himself came under the influence of the Oxford atmosphere and used biological analogies, which, although wholly inappropriate and misleading, captured the popular imagination in the seventies of last century. For the reference to Tylor's doctrine as " evolution " revealed a singular inability to understand the meaning of a simple biological term, the more exact parallel being the claim for

* *The History of America*, vol. i. book 4.

" spontaneous generation," with all its unfortunate implications of errors of observation and mistaken interpretation. However, Tylor's version of the teaching of Bastian, with its misleading labels " evolution " and " animism," was adopted far and wide, and provided the jargon that for more than half a century did duty for serious argument and inhibited real investigation. Freud and his disciples eagerly accepted this ethnological teaching as the true gospel, the prophets of which were Sir James Fraser, of *The Golden Bough*, and Professor Wundt, the author of *Völkerpsychologie*. For if the ethnologists were able to assure Freud and his followers that scattered peoples had independently the one of the other devised the same myths and folk-tales, then the reality of " typical symbols " was proved. Not only so, but the field was open for the Freudians to repay the ethnologists by explaining what their identical beliefs and myths really mean ! Hence Freud, Abraham, Rank, and the rest of them began to provide the world with such striking demonstrations of *reductio ad absurdum* as *Totem and Taboo*, *Dreams and Myths*, *The Birth of the Hero*, *inter alia*, and Jung to write about " the collective unconscious " and the phylogeny of symbols. What renders all this speculation so obviously futile is that none of these writers has taken the trouble to go to first-hand sources for his

information, for had he done so the baseless-
ness of his pretended explanations could not
have failed to become patent. Instead of
this, the Freudians are satisfied to get their
ethnological information second-hand from
the writings of Sir James Fraser and Wundt,
two authors deeply committed to the Bastian-
Tylor fallacy.

The importance of the article by Dr Rivers
is that it sketches the history of a movement
to destroy the fallacies of supposed independent evolutions of custom and belief by
proving that in ancient times, as at present,
knowledge and men's interpretation of their
experience were diffused abroad throughout
the world. The common features of myths
and folk-tales are not expressions of instinct
or "the collective unconscious," nor are
they "typical symbols." They are due to
the diffusion from one centre of an arbitrary
tale which had a definite history differing
vastly from that postulated by either Freud
or Jung.

Made in the USA
Middletown, DE
17 June 2023